CYCLING PARADISES

Designed and produced by Olo Éditions
www.oloeditions.com

EDITORIAL DIRECTION: Nicolas Marçais
ART DIRECTION: Philippe Marchand
EDITOR: Sara Quémener
ENGLISH TRANSLATION: Roland Glasser
GRAPHIC DESIGN: Émilie Greenberg/Emigreen
LAYOUT: Élise Godmuse
INFOGRAPHICS: Émilie Greenberg / Emigreen, Élise Godmuse and Aurélie Lequeux
IMAGE EDITING: Cédric Delsart
COPYEDITING: Catherine Decayeux

US COVER DESIGN: Kayleigh Jankowski

First published in the United States of America in 2018 by
Universe Publishing, a division of
Rizzoli International Publications, Inc.
300 Park Avenue South
New York, NY 10010
www.rizzoliusa.com

Originally published in French in 2017 by Olo Éditions
© 2017, Olo Éditions

2018 2019 2020 2021 / 10 9 8 7 6 5 4 3 2 1

ISBN: 978-0-7893-3386-5

Library of Congress Control Number: 2018944710

Printed in Malaysia

CYCLING PARADISES

*100 Bike Tours of the World's
Most Breathtaking Places to Pedal*

CLAUDE DROUSSENT

UNIVERSE

So what's heaven for you?

It's not easy to choose the most beautiful cycling spots, the ones that dreams are made of. Such experiences are so personal, frequently dating back many years. True cycling paradise is often the very start, that point when your parent first let go and watched you pedal away on your own—wobbling perhaps—to explore your neighborhood or that quiet trail into the forest. Moments of freedom like those are simply unforgettable. But we had to choose our favorite cycling spots, and that involved a great deal of subjectivity.

These one hundred most scenic locations, sites, and routes truly offer something for everyone— whatever your cycling ability or interest. Our task was mostly about elimination, because there were thousands of possible candidates across the planet. And, indeed, that is what we found most striking: the extent to which, in the early twenty-first century, the humble bicycle has become such a universal object. In many countries, the bicycle is an essential means of transportation for those who can't afford other means of getting around, whereas in the developed world, the bicycle has become fashionable again after being sidelined in the 1960s in favor of the car. City stockbrokers ride "fixies" along the Thames, and businessmen and lawyers compete over Tour de France mountain passes or on the most stunning trails in the Rocky Mountains or Hong Kong. In the United States, there is talk of a "new golf," but with added fitness benefits. Bicycle touring, meanwhile, is now called "bikepacking."

We wanted these one hundred cycling spots to cover all the continents, because you can even cycle in Antarctica! We divided them into four chapters reflecting the four main types of cycling: road biking, mountain biking, city cycling, and the contemplative adventuring of bicycle touring. Perhaps you too have dreamed of pedaling in Alaska, or through the jungle of Bali, or on the slopes of a volcano in Hawaii? Maybe you've wondered what it would be like to ride round Iceland or Manhattan, to lose yourself in Siberia or the Rwandan hills, or ride up Mount Tamalpais, where the mountain bike was invented? Whatever your preference, cycling is all about encounters, shared experiences, and, of course, exploration—something that cycling enables more than any other means of transportation.

These one hundred cycling paradises serve merely to inspire you to ride out and explore, to nurture and fuel a passion for adventure, and to throw a leg over the top tube and pedal off—be it to challenge yourself or simply see what's around that bend in the road.

Claude Droussent

Contents

Road

Mountain

008　　　　**058**

City

Touring

See you at the Barry-Roubaix!

Cross the Golden Gate Bridge, and you'll discover a terrain ripe for new experiences. It was here, around Mount Tamalpais, that the mountain bike was born. This then birthed the "gravel," a hybrid that combines the best of both worlds. It is as effective on asphalt as it is on trails, such as the Old Railroad Grade, which winds around Tamalpais. The gravel trend has become so strong in the United States that, in 2009, a bunch of guys organized the first Barry-Roubaix, which takes place in Michigan.

THE 18-MILE (30 KM) HEADLANDS LOOP
The classic route for San Francisco roadies

1 Bridge Cafe (for a snack)

2 Hawk Hill (viewpoint)

3 The Lone Sailor Memorial (statue)

4 Presidio : Arguello Gate (viewpoint)

5 Velo Rouge Cafe (for refreshments)

California dreams *San Francisco, United States*

San Francisco is a real cycling city, as much as Chicago, New York, and Portland. Hipsters on "fixies" make child's play of the steepest streets, but there is also a large and dynamic community of roadies, sporty types in spandex who take the most impressive escape route out of town—the Golden Gate Bridge—in search of the beautiful roads on the other side in Marin County. A two-way cycle path leads across the iconic span, and then a few pedal turns take you up to a viewpoint that offers a stunning panorama over San Francisco and the Bay, including the little island of Alcatraz and its famous former penitentiary. If you get there early enough—and the fog has deigned to disperse—you can enjoy the sunrise over the Bay, which is a wonder to behold. Sniff the eucalyptus-scented air and then pick one of the many possible itineraries, lasting one to two hours. If you're looking for a sporty challenge, then head north on a loop via Hawk Hill or else by way of the Col du Pantoll. Paradise Loop, on the Tiburon Peninsula farther east, is less difficult but just as easy on the eye. You can even take the aptly named Golden Gate Ferry back to the city.

Boulder, the true capital

It may not have the atmosphere of Copenhagen or even San Francisco, but Boulder—100,000 inhabitants, 30 miles (50 km) northwest of Denver—is undoubtedly the medium-sized city with the most-developed cycling culture in the world. Located 5,430 feet (1,655 m) above sea level, Boulder has strong environmental credentials (first local carbon tax, in 2007), a thriving outdoor scene, and a sizable proportion of young people—the city is home to the flagship University of Colorado. It's impossible to count the number of bike shops or cycling champions. Pure delight!

PIKES PEAK, A CLIMB WORTH TACKLING

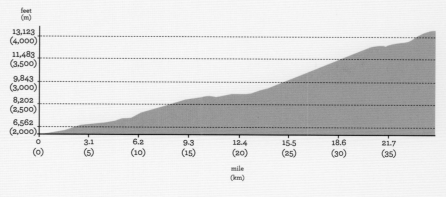

Thrills at the summit *Pikes Peak, United States*

Pikes Peak is part of cycling fantasy, just like Mont Ventoux in France, partly because the road is closed to bicycles, except for one day a year in late summer, and partly because this summit in the Rocky Mountains bears the name of a legendary automobile hill climb. If you've got the guts to line up for the annual Ride Pikes Peak alongside a few hundred other foolhardy cyclists—and, above all, make it to the finish—you'll get a sense of the thrills experienced by the car drivers. Pikes Peak is not a mountain pass, but instead a superb dead-end road built a century ago into the red rock. Its surface is in perfect condition, but it has 162 bends—many of them hairpins or blind corners—with vertiginous precipices lacking the slightest protection. The climb begins at Manitou Springs, which is 60 miles (100 km) south of Denver. We're already at more than 7,500 feet (2,300 m) above sea level. The summit lies at 14,110 feet (4,275 m), with 6,500 feet (2,000 m) of climbing to be accomplished in 24 miles (39 km). The second part of the climb, across a bare landscape, is dreadfully tough. Here, the average gradient is 9%, the oxygen is thin, and the cool air can suddenly gust. Pikes Peak by bike is a monstrous sporting challenge.

650 feet (200 m) of cobblestones at 33%!

American cyclists are nothing if not ingenious. In Los Angeles, Fargo Street has 390 feet (120 m) at an average gradient of 34%. According to the Strava app, the record is 7.5 mph (12 km/h). In Pittsburgh, Pennsylvania, riders compete on Canton Avenue with its 650 feet (200 m) of cobblestones at 33%, which puts the Koppenberg climb in Belgium to shame! In late November, the Dirty Dozen race covers the steepest hills in the city—all of them similar in profile.

MOUNT WASHINGTON, A CHALLENGE FOR CLIMBERS

7⅓ miles
(11.8 km) of climbing

11.9%
average gradient

19%
maximum gradient

4,698 feet
(1,432 m) altitude gain

Presidential *Mount Washington, United States*

You don't expect to find this type of difficulty, halfway between Boston and Montreal, in New Hampshire. Mount Washington rises to 6,288 feet (1,916 m) and is the highest summit in the Presidential Range of the modest White Mountains, part of the northern Appalachians. "Presidential" is an apt descriptor for the single road that leads to the summit. Steep slopes fall away, offering grandiose views as far as the Atlantic coast of Maine, which is

60 miles away. There are similarities with Pikes Peak, its taller Colorado cousin: a panoramic route, a gravel section, and also a ban on bicycles. The toll road is only open to extreme sports lovers two days a year in summer, for a practice and the official hill climb. No more than six hundred entrants are allowed; you must be fast to sign up. Nevertheless, the most difficult thing is hauling yourself above the Great Gulf—a glacial cirque that marks the edge of the tree

line—on D-day. Even in summer, the notoriously erratic weather can turn this climb into one of the toughest on the planet. In 1934, a wind speed of 231 mph (372 km/h) was recorded at the summit, a world record for many decades.

Home of the Ironman

The Ironman—comprising a 2.4-mile (4 km) swim, followed by a 112-mile (180 km) bicycle ride, and then a marathon, was conceived in Hawaii in 1978. Ironman remains the most famous triathlon in the world. The hilly cycling course runs along the west coast of the island from Kailua-Kona to Kapaau and back again. Controversial cyclist Lance Armstrong won the short version (Ironman 70.3 Hawaii) in 2012, at the age of forty, before being banned from all competition.

MAUNA KEA: THE SLOPE TO CLIMB ON HAWAII

68°F
(20°C)
average temperature
difference between
Hilo and the summit

4h46m
record for the
section from Hilo to
Mauna Kea

6%
average gradient

20%
maximum gradient,
at the top of the
volcano

Objective: Moon *Mauna Kea, Hawaii, United States*

Mauna Kea is a dormant volcano and the highest summit (13,803 feet / 4,207 m) in the Hawaiian archipelago. It lies on the Big Island, 2,484 miles (4,000 km) from Los Angeles. Mauna Kea has been sacred to the native Hawaiians for centuries. Since the 1960s, the summit has been home to a number of observatories because it is one of the best sites in the world for astronomical observations, owing to the arid conditions, the deep darkness provided by the archipelago's isolation in the middle of the Pacific, and the fact that the cloud cover remains mostly below the summit. More recently, Mauna Kea has become a destination for adventurous cyclists. A hybrid bike of the gravel type is recommended, because the route includes a long section of dirt trail. The single road starts in Hilo, by the ocean, and comprises 42 miles (69 km) of continuous climbing. By comparison with several Alpine climbs, its height difference is four times that of Alpe-d'Huez, its gravel section (4.3 miles / 7 km) is the same as the Colle delle Finestre, and its fiercest slopes are comparable with those of the Zoncolan. Add the altitude to that—along with rock falls, accounts of lava flows, and an Alpine landscape—and the Hawaiian paradise becomes a hell. Two-thirds of the astronomers on Mauna Kea suffer from altitude sickness.

Ride to Castro's bedroom

It's a tough expedition, but Pico Turquino can be tackled in a day by mountain bike fitted with a suspension and disc brakes (the trails are demanding in both directions). When you leave Bayamo, in the center of the island, you soon find yourself in the jungle. Don't miss the Comandancia de la Plata, Fidel Castro's secret headquarters during the Cuban Revolution. The buildings are intact, and you can even visit the bedroom of *el lider maximo*!

VISIT HAVANA TO A SALSA BEAT
A relaxed excursion, *a la cubana,* to explore the capital

- ● Old Havana > Malecón seafront esplanade
- ● Malecón seafront esplanade > Vedado business district
- ○ Vedado business district > Christopher Columbus Cemetery
- ● Christopher Columbus Cemetery > Lenin Park
- ● Lenin Park > Botanical Garden
- ○ Botanical Garden > Barrio Chino
- ● Barrio Chino > return to Old Havana

Duration
6h

Distance
21 miles (35 km)

Difficulty
low

Rentals
rutabikes.com

Che's mountain *Sierra Maestra, Cuba*

The road skirts the turquoise Caribbean Sea along the island's south coast to Santiago, some 500 miles (800 km) from Havana. The urn containing Fidel Castro's ashes was interred in the cemetery of Santiago, the cradle of the Cuban Revolution. You won't be able to resist visiting this spot, which has become a place of pilgrimage. The trip starts with a superb 125-mile (200 km) ride along the Nacional 20 from Niquero. The crystal clear waters, which boast some sumptuous dive spots farther out, are on the right of a corniche, a joy in itself. The imposing peaks, curves, and forests of the Sierra Maestra provide a backdrop to the left. Castro, Che Guevara, and their *barbudos* hid out here during their years of struggle in the 1950s. Halfway through the ride, you'll see Pico Turquino, which is Cuba's highest point at 6,476 feet (1,974 m). The Nacional 20 to Santiago Bay is not a very busy road. It's often narrow, and in places, it shows damage from hurricanes. Bear in mind the words of Columbus upon "discovering" Cuba in 1492: "It's the most beautiful land a man can see with his own eyes." Indeed, it is a very beautiful land to explore by pedal power, in 86°F (30°C) heat, with a light breeze.

Glory to Victor Hugo!

Colombian cyclists have made their mark on the Tour de France. Luis "Lucho" Herrera was the first national cycling hero in the 1980s, wearing the iconic polka-dot jersey. Nairo Quintana is his country's contemporary hero, having mounted the podium in Paris on three occasions between 2013 and 2016. Curiously, until 2017, only one Colombian had ever worn the yellow jersey: Victor Hugo Peña, a lanky six-footer who wasn't even a climber! He wore the famous colors for three days during the 2003 Tour de France.

55 MILES (90 KM) AROUND TUNJA

- Tunja > Sora (9 miles/15 km)
- Sora > Villa de Leyva on the Via Chiquiza (25 miles/40 km)
- Villa de Leyva > Samacá (40 miles/65 km)
- Samacá > The Bridge of Boyacá (46 miles/75 km)
- The Bridge of Boyacá > Tunja (55 miles/90 km)

Duration
4 to 5h

Difficulty
high

Repair
Ciclo Standar,
in Tunja

Recommended pit stop
Pastelería Francesa
or Matilde Blain
in Villa de Leyva

Riding after the beetles Tunja, Colombia

Los escarabajos, or "the beetles," has been the nickname given to Colombian cyclists ever since their first appearance in the Tour de France in the 1980s. They earned this sobriquet because of their stick-thin thighs and arms that belied a diabolical climbing ability. To understand a little about how they developed these talents, you could do worse than ride around Tunja, capital of the Boyacá department and the highest city in Colombia, at 9,127 feet

(2,820 m). It's a university town, cultural center, and seat of Amerindian heritage. Nairo Quintana, the cycling champion of the 2010s, grew up in the neighboring town of Cómbita. Like others before him, Quitana cycled to school and back every day, which partly explains his talents. The terrain is never flat. The hills of San Lazaro—"mountain of the hanged"—and of the La Pirgua botanical garden are impressive promontories reaching more than

9,000 feet (3,000 m). Acclimatization is no easy task for an organism used to living at sea level. In the course of a 55-mile (90 km) route from Tunja to Villa de Leyva—a former colonial town that still has cobbled streets—and back, the altitude constantly varies between 6,800 (2,100 m) and 9,500 feet (2,900 m). The climbs are not particularly high in gradient, but they seem never-ending. This is where the kids of Colombia become *escarabajos*.

A halt at the hospice

The Hospice du Col du Saint-Gothard, which was built in 1237, was renovated recently. It originally provided rudimentary lodgings to pilgrims and lost travelers. There are several similar buildings elsewhere in the Alps, such as the Hospice du Grand-Saint-Bernard (8,100 feet/2,473 m)—the first parts of which were constructed in 1050—and the Hospice du Simplon (6,500 feet/2,000 m). These buildings of the past are now all shelters available to cyclists worn out by the mountains.

FIVE OTHER SUBLIME MOUNTAIN PASSES IN SWITZERLAND

❶ Col de la Croix - 5,833 feet (1,776 m)
From Villars-sur-Ollon to Les Diablerets,
11 miles, with some tough gradients

❷ Grosse Scheidegg - 6,437 feet (1,962 m)
In the Bernese Highlands, start from
Grindenwald, with the Eiger in front of you

❸ Susten - 7,415 feet (2,224 m)
Canton of Uri, in the center of Switzerland,
10½ miles from Wassen

❹ Col du Sanetsch - 7,356 feet (2,251 m)
To the north of Sion, a quite remote climb,
descend by cable car

❺ Albula - 7,596 feet (2,315 m)
14 miles of climbing to the north of Saint-Moritz

The scenic route   *Col du Saint-Gothard, Switzerland*

They call it *la vecchia tremola* ("the shaky old lady"). They speak Italian on this side of the Saint-Gothard because it lies in the canton of Ticino. The climb is unlike any other, which makes it the favorite of many Swiss cyclists who are used to slogging away in the mountains. From Airolo, at the bottom, to the top of the Saint-Gothard, at 6,909 feet (2,108 m), it's only 8 miles (13 km) of climbing at a relatively comfortable average gradient of 7.4%.

But *la vecchia tremola* holds other delights, starting with its 24 extremely tight bends, which are concentrated in two distinct sections that make for a most spectacular route up the side of the mountain. Then there's the road surface of small cobblestones, constructed nearly two hundred years ago, hence the "shaky," even if it's not nearly as rough a ride as the notorious Trench of Arenberg, which features in the Paris-Roubaix. Still, it's unique!

Toward the top, the landscape becomes pretty rocky, and a lake marks the summit. The ambiance is surprisingly calm. There are other ways to traverse the Saint-Gothard: a road tunnel; a rail tunnel; and a wide, recently constructed dual carriageway—the traffic hum of which is sometimes audible as you pedal skyward over cobblestones, far from everything, or nearly.

Land of the descenders

Each January, the most famous downhill ski race takes place on the Hahnenkamm (or "Cockscomb") opposite the south face of the Horn in the Kitzbühel Alps. Skiers reach top speeds of 87 mph (140 km/h) as they shoot down the Streif course, which is somewhat faster than the 66.5 mph (107 km/h) attained by the Australian cyclist Mark Renshaw on the descent of the Tourmalet in 2015, an unofficial record for a Tour de France.

28
bends

3,116 feet
(950 m) altitude gain
in 4.66 miles (7.5 km)

13%
average gradient

22.3%
maximum gradient

Monster of the Tyrol *Kitzbüheler Horn, Austria*

The Kitzbüheler Horn is not a climb familiar to fans of the Tour de France or the Giro d'Italia. Those who have attempted it by bike retain strong yet mixed memories of extreme suffering and huge pride. It would be fair to say that the Horn is the most demanding challenge on a road bike on the European continent. It's not its length—barely six miles—that makes it stand out, but the brutal way that the slope kicks up as soon as you leave

Kitzbühel, with its gothic churches and luxury boutiques. Stop by the side of the road on the right at the Kitzbühel Challenge machine and take a ticket that will provide a record of the performance to come. From then on it's hell on your thighs, heart, and lungs. The bucolic backdrop of the Tyrol encourages a sense of tranquility; it's a delusion. There is not a moment of respite on this asphalt as it winds through the alpine pastures. You must

maintain a steely mindset in the face of the signs that indicate the gradient is 18.21%. The official climb ends at 5,479 feet (1,670 m) at the Gipfelhaus, where you hand in your ticket. You can then continue along a private trail that leads to the TV tower at 6,549 feet (1,996 m). It's a little more pain, but you'll be rewarded with a 360-degree view over the dazzling Alps.

The Vikings and the Tour de France

Fewer than twenty Norwegians have ever participated in the Tour de France. A few, such as the veteran Thor Hushovd, have shone. Perhaps they remind the Norwegian fans of their much-adored cross-country skiers, who are also a tough bunch. These fans have developed a passion for the Tour and can be seen in large numbers along the route. The Arctic Race of Norway—the most northerly race in the world—began in 2013. It is held in the region around Bodo and Narvik, opposite the Lofoten Islands.

THE LOFOTEN ISLANDS

5
main islands
(at least 19
square miles /
50 km²)

55.4°F
(13°C) average
summer
temperature

45
polar days
in June and July
at Svolvær

3,760 feet
(1,146 m) height of
the highest summit,
Higravstind

Midnight sun *Lofoten Islands, Norway*

As everyone knows, Norway is the land of fjords, offering breathtaking climbs up the sides of those many ancient glacial valleys with their impressive peaks. But why not take the opposite stance? Take advantage of the midnight sun—from late May to mid-July—and do some thrilling touring on the flat. The direction will be to the Lofoten Islands, 190 miles (300 km) above the Arctic Circle. It's an incredible landscape to ride through; even just the pretty

European Route E10 as it snakes along the narrow coastal strip between the mountains and the sea. The Lofoten Islands are linked by bridges or tunnels. It doesn't rain here in summer, and you can ride under the famous midnight sun for three or four days, or as long as you wish. A vehicle with supplies is a good idea. Take the ferry from Bodo to the island of Moskenesøya. The trip starts at the village of Å—the most southerly point on this exploration of the Lofoten

Islands—and continues via Ballstad (and the short Nusfjord ferry crossing), then Gimsoysand with its lovely beach, Henningsvær ("Venice of the Lofoten"), Svolvær, Fiskebol, and even as far as Andenes at the northern tip of the Vesterålen district. It offers nearly 200 miles (300 km) of fishing hamlets, colorful cabins, natural wonders of rock and plant, and even art galleries.

The Puy de Dôme, one day a year

If the narrow road through the Verdon Gorge remains relatively unknown to cyclists, it's partly because the Tour de France is simply too large for it. Likewise, it will never again ride to the top of the legendary Puy de Dôme, which lies six miles (9.7 km) from Clermont-Ferrand. A rack railway, the Panoramique des Dômes, was laid over the road in 1992. There is a service road, but it's open to cyclists only one Sunday in June.

CYCLE THE VERDON CANYON

The most beautiful viewpoints on this 46-mile (75 km) loop,
starting from the junction of the D90 and the D71

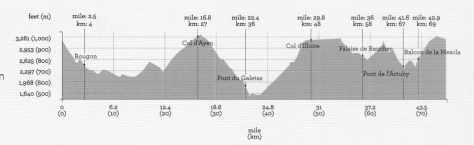

A canyon in Provence *Verdon Gorge, France*

The French Alps offer a vast catalogue of cycling dreams, the best known of which are the Galibier and Izoard passes, and Alpe d'Huez. The Verdon Gorge is mentioned much more rarely. This exceptional site in the Provence Alps is best known to rock climbers, bungee jumpers, and canoeists/ kayakers. Its sublime corniche is a wonder to cycle. You can tackle it from the west via the pretty villages of Moustiers-Sainte-Marie, or from the east via Castellane and its imposing cliff, Le Roc. Alternatively, start as close as possible to the actual loop of the gorge, a route that offers the most attractive of compromises: the need for physical commitment, with endless climbs and descents of between 1,300 feet (400 m) and 3,280 feet (1,000 m), and the reward of so many breathtaking views. From the Route des Crêtes above La Palud to the south slope after Aiguines, you're forever tempted to get as close as possible to the edge of the precipice of the "Grand Canyon of Europe" and the blue-green waters of the Verdon. The river is sometimes more than 2,000 feet (700 m) below. The views are as bewitching as the incredible geological phenomenon that carved out this gorge from the limestone rock. It's a vertiginous, magical experience.

If you've never climbed the Mûr...

Competitive cycling has always been wildly popular in Brittany. No one can consider themselves worthy of such champions as Louison Bobet or Bernard Hinault if they haven't climbed the Mûr-de-Bretagne, right in the center of the region, without flagging. It's a straight course, barely 1.25 miles (2 km) long with gradients of up to 15%, lined with trees—and several rows of spectators when the Tour de France takes this route.

A LOVELY RIDE ALONG THE CHANNEL
Two hundred fifty miles (400 km) along the magnificent north coast of Brittany, following the start of the EuroVelo 4 cycle route that goes all the way to Kiev, Ukraine

Roscoff
mile: 0
(km: 0)

Morlaix
mile: 19.3
(km: 31)

Plestin-les-Grèves
mile: 47.2
(km: 76)

Lannion
mile: 62.1
(km: 100)

Perros-Guirec
mile: 85.1
(km: 137)

Paimpol
mile: 112.5
(km: 181)

Saint-Brieuc
mile: 149.1
(km: 240)

Erquy
mile: 172.1
(km: 277)

Saint-Malo
mile: 192.6
(km: 310)

Le Mont-Saint-Michel
mile: 236.1
(km: 380)

Brittany trails *Pays de Léon, France*

The Côte des Légendes in northwest Brittany is a place of strange encounters: sumptuous light bathing bare landscapes, fishermen, kelping boats, a seventeenth-century guardhouse constructed between two rocky outcrops (at Meneham), animal-shaped granite blocks beside a fine sandy beach, and cyclists whizzing past on the trails. These trails go by a special name in the Pays de Léon: *ribinoù* (singular: *ribin*). They are composed of

earth and crushed stone, with a strip of grass down the middle. They were made by and for the area's farmers and their tractors. In the 1980s, local son and Paris-Roubaix fan Jean-Paul Mellouët, who sported a druid look, had the idea for a race along these *ribinoù*: the Tro Bro Léon, which would also serve to raise funds for a school that was part of the Diwan network, which was set up to promote the Breton language, his other interest. The Tro Bro

Léon has become a fixture on the professional circuit. Jean-Paul Mellouët is also as much responsible for the gravel trend of the 2010s as the promoters of the Eroica and Strade Bianche events in Tuscany. Everyone should ride the *ribinoù* at least once, wind along the edge of the *abers* — fjords without the steep cliffs that are unbelievably charming — before tucking into a dish of *kig ha farz*, the local stew. Invigorating!

Funny records

Among the cosmopolitan population of pretenders to the Ventoux crown, there are some original characters who haunt the summer streets of Bédoin in spandex. Some belong to the Club des Cinglés du Ventoux (Ventoux Crazies Club), which gives some idea of their mettle. Others are holders of some pretty extreme records. In 2006, Jean-Pascal Roux climbed the monster 11 times in 24 hours. Betty Kals holds the women's record of eight ascents in 24 hours, in 2015.

THE THREE ROUTES UP MONT VENTOUX

● Malaucène > Mont Ventoux 14 miles (22 km)   ● Bédoin > Mont Ventoux 14 miles (22 km)   ● Sault > Mont Ventoux 16 miles (26 km)

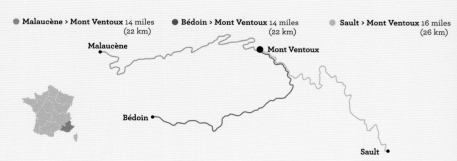

Tour de force *Mont Ventoux, France*

The descent of Mont Ventoux is exhilarating for sure, but any accomplished cyclist fantasizes about tackling the "Giant of Provence" in the other direction. There are many reasons, including the media coverage of the Tour de France, of course, and also the memory of Tom Simpson's tragic death in 1967, and the unparalleled configuration of this 6,272-foot (1,912 m) high mountain that stands quite separate from the Alps and is visible for more than 60 miles (100 km) away in clear conditions—although the weather around its summit can be quite capricious. Finally, there's the vast stretch of limestone scree covering its upper reaches, which is as disturbing as it is seductive. Let's be quite clear: you can't pride yourself on having climbed Mont Ventoux unless you take the hardest and most demanding slope, which starts at Bédoin. Aim for at least 1,900 miles (3,000 km) of training. You won't regret it once you reach the bend at Saint-Estève, where you enter the forest. Here the road kicks up to an average gradient of 9% over a relentless 5.5 miles (9 km) until Chalet-Reynard, where the scenery changes. The last 4 miles (6 km) snake through a "lunar landscape." Mont Ventoux is a lesson in humility, patience, and determination. When you attain the summit, you feel like you've conquered a legend. In fine weather, you're also rewarded with sublime views. Quite unforgettable!

Paris or not?

Every year, the Paris-Roubaix race starts from Compiègne, which is 50 miles (80 km) north of the capital. The reason for this geographical shift is that it's not easy to find cobbled stretches of road in northern France, where the remnants are cherished and maintained like national monuments. If the race began farther south, the route would be much too long. Paris used to play a pivotal role in the cycling calendar, but it now hosts only one major annual event: the finish of the Tour de France on the welcoming cobbles of the Champs-Élysées.

VALENCIENNES TO ROUBAIX
Your challenge: ride the last 60 miles (100 km) of the "Queen of the Classics"

- ● Valenciennes >
  Trench of Arenberg
- ● Trench of Arenberg > Warlaing
- ● Warlaing > Abattoirs Trail

- ● Abattoirs Trail >
  Mons-en-Pévèle
- ● Mons-en-Pévèle > Carrefour de l'Arbre
- ● Carrefour de l'Arbre > Roubaix

Duration
4 to 5h, depending on breaks

Difficulty
very high

Breaks
Orchies, Templeuve-en-Pévèle, and the café at the Carrefour de l'Arbre

Tip
Return by train, from Lille Flandres to Valenciennes

Riding the cobbles *Trench of Arenberg, France*

Every second Sunday in April at 2 p.m., families gather around their TV screens to watch cycling's springtime High Mass. Dubbed "the Hell of the North," Paris-Roubaix is a source of hysteria. The final 60 miles (100 km) are the worst for those still in contention, because what follows is no ordinary difficulty. Indeed, it is notorious in cycling culture. Called the "Wallers-Arenberg Trench," or simply the "Trench of Arenberg" by riders, the media, and fans, the official name for this straight 7,874-foot (2,400 m) stretch of cobblestones through the Raismes-Saint-Amand-Wallers Forest, which is closed to traffic, is Drève des Boules d'Hérin. It was the former professional cyclist Jean Stablinski who suggested its inclusion in the Paris-Roubaix course during the 1960s. He remembered having taken the route as a boy on the way to work at the mine, his first job. The Trench of Arenberg is disjointed and badly aligned, giving both rider and bike a good shaking. It's almost impossible to hold a consistent line, even if you tackle it at full speed, and the first section is a falsely flat downhill. On race day, barriers prevent riders from taking the verge, although the ordinary cyclist will find it provides some respite.

Balearics or Canaries?

Two Spanish archipelagos 1,300 miles (2,000 km) apart compete for the attention of European cyclists seeking warm weather. Out in the Atlantic, the Canaries enjoy a half-tropical, half-desert climate—the Sahara is not far away. You can ride across each of the islands, from Tenerife to Lanzarote, without running the risk of boredom, and you can climb pretty high—up to 8,858 feet (2,700 m)—to the foot of the volcano Mount Teide. The cliffs of Majorca on the Mediterranean, however, have more charm than the beaches of the Canaries.

MAJORCA: THE LOVELIEST SPOTS ON THE WEST COAST

❶ Start here, between Banyalbufar and Andratx

❷ Climb the little passes of Galilea and Puigpunyent, to the west of Palma, starting out from Calvià

❸ From the charming village of Bunyola, 8.7 miles (14 km) to the Cuber and Gorg Blau reservoirs (60 hairpins!)

❹ The most beautiful road on the island, which starts from a little port and climbs to 2,000 feet (600 m)

❺ Cycle as far as the Albercutx watchtower via Pollença beach and the rocky inlet of Figuera

Cosmopolitan isle *Majorca, Balearic Islands, Spain*

More than any other island in the Mediterranean, Majorca has embraced cycling as a solution to the mass tourism that began in the 1960s, and given itself a new image to fit with the times. As soon as you leave Palma, where nearly half of the island's 860,000 inhabitants live, you're struck by the multitude of people in spandex on the roads, with helmets on their heads, in small groups as well as large pelotons. Many of them are speaking English and

German. It's a year-round phenomenon because it never gets very cold in Majorca (an average of 60°F/16°C in January) or too hot. There are countless agencies that organize cycling tours here; the Irish champion Stephen Roche was one of the first. With its almond and strawberry trees, the island offers the twin attractions of quality training for accomplished sportspeople and a paradise for more contemplative folk. Its most picturesque surprises are

to be found in the west of the island in the low mountains of the Serra de Tramuntana, which are named after the *tramuntana*, a chill wind that blows from the north. Here, you can find jewels such as Sa Calobra, a 6-mile (10 km) ascent with majestic curves. You'll rarely climb it alone.

The Snowdon guide

Until the turn of the century, sports cycling was still rather niche in the United Kingdom. Now though, there are "MAMILs" (middle-aged men in Lycra) everywhere, while riders such as Froome and Wiggins have won some of the biggest races in the international cycling calendar. Their mentor, Dave Brailsford, grew up in Snowdonia and sometimes returns to the roads on which he once trained. His favorite is a circuit of Mount Snowdon, which starts at his village of Deiniolen, then returns via the magnificent Llanberis Pass. Pure joy.

LE VÉLO AU ROYAUME-UNI

3.9%
of men
travel to work by bicycle

4
million people
pedal at least once a week

3.5
million bicycles
were sold in 2015

1
million women
cycling by 2020 is the aim of Breeze, an initiative supported by the UK National Lottery

Welsh gem *Snowdonia National Park, United Kingdom*

Neighboring England is envious. None of its regions, not even the superb Yorkshire Dales, can rival the cycling gem that is Snowdonia National Park in North Wales. Located 70 miles (113km) southwest of Liverpool, Snowdonia gives a first impression of a wild, arid place, but it is quite fascinating. The United Kingdom is not somewhere that you would expect to find high-mountain flora, such as the Snowdon lily—which otherwise is found only in the Alps and the Rockies—or see a soaring osprey. The sunny coast is nicknamed "the Welsh Riviera." Snowdonia boasts nearly one hundred peaks more than 2,000 feet (600 m) high, with Snowdon being the highest mountain in England and Wales at 3,560 feet (1,085 m). Amid this concentration of varied landscapes—coasts, lakes, summits, glacial valleys, and forests—you'll find quiet roads with a smooth surface. You never get bored here. Indeed, you might even be surprised to find a hairpin at 25% gradient on a climb. Amazement is all around, from Aberdovey in the south—where the famous Cambrian Coast Sportive starts and finishes each September—to the valleys of Carnedd Llywelyn in the north.

A museum for an annex

Fiorenzo Magni was an Italian champion of the 1940s and '50s. He was the "third man" of the golden age of Italian cycling, which was marked by the rivalry between Fausto Coppi and Gino Bartali. He had such fondness for the chapel at Ghisallo that he dedicated his final years (he died in 2012 at age 91) to the creation of a cycling museum adjoining it. This small museum displays various cycling artifacts and photographs, as well as donations from the champions of today, for which the chapel no longer has room.

TO THE ROOTS OF THE CAMPIONNISSIMI
The places where Italy's cycling champions grew up

❶ Piedmont:
Costante Girardengo, Fausto Coppi, Giuseppe Saronni

❷ Lombardy:
Learco Guerra, Alfredo Binda, Gianni Motta, Felice Gimondi, Gianni Bugno, Claudio Chiappucci, Ivan Basso

❸ Trentino:
Francesco Moser, Maurizio Fondriest

❹ Emilia-Romagna:
Ercole Baldini, Marco Pantani

❺ Tuscany: Gino Bartali, Fiorenzo Magni, Gastone Nencini, Mario Cipollini, Paolo Bettini

❻ Sicily:
Vincenzo Nibali

Under the Madonna's protection *Ghisallo, Italy*

The notion of religion and the sacred is never far from the image of self-sacrifice required in professional cycling, at least on the part of its champions. If you were to look for a place or mountain to fit this idea, you might list Ghisallo (Lombardy) in the cosseted atmosphere of Lake Como at the top. Starting from Bellagio—a pearl nestling between the two arms of the lake—the climb to Ghisallo is dead south: 6 miles (10 km), the first four of which have gradients as high as 14% in places. It's a spiritual journey leading to the chapel of the Madonna. According to legend, Ghisallo was a seventeenth-century gentleman who was attacked by brigands and was saved only by an image of the Virgin Mary that he saw at a nearby shrine. Here, we are at relatively low altitude: 2,473 feet (754 m). When the first editions of the Tour of Lombardy came this way in the 1920s (the road was cobbled), the priest of Ghisallo rang the bells as the riders passed; this became a tradition. In 1949, Pope Pius XII declared the Madonna of Ghisallo to be the patron saint of cyclists. The Ghisallo may not always be decisive in the outcome of the Tour of Lombardy—the most romantic of cycling races—but it still remains a key challenge that is climbed each year in a spirit of joy and elation.

Lisbon to Compostela

There are many routes stretching across Europe to Santiago de Compostela, . Some of them can be cycled. The Portuguese have created the concept of *bicigrinos*, or bicycling pilgrims. The route from Lisbon to the holy site in Galicia is a marked road via Coimbra, Porto, and Pontevedra in Spain—370 miles (590 km) in all. It looks simple enough on the map—a straight road due north—yet there is a total of 19,600 feet (6,000 m) of climbing. Still, there are many welcoming *gîtes* (holiday homes available for rent) along the way where you can spend the night.

SAGA OF THE PORTUGUESE CHAMPIONS

Antonio Barbosa
was the first Portuguese cyclist to take part in the Tour de France in 1956

Acacio Da Silva
wore the yellow jersey for three days in 1989

Joaquim Agostinho
finished third in the Tour de France on two occasions: 1977 and 1979

Rui Costa
was the World Road Cycling Champion in 2013

First star *Serra da Estrela, Portugal*

Portugal has a strong cycling culture with terrain to match. In the far south, the foothills of the Algarve are quite attractive outside of the summer season, as are the Azores in the Atlantic. There is one lesser-known route that is well worth the ride: the Serra da Estrela (Star Mountain), the highest mountain range in Continental Portugal, even if they had to add a 23-foot (7 m) tower to its peak to reach 6,561 feet (2,000 m). Located in the northeast of the country, halfway between Lisbon and Porto, this hunk of granite boasts some unexpected alpine landscapes. The climb from Covilha via the quiet regional road 339 winds through rosemary and juniper bushes before reaching rockier territory. It's not unusual to see a golden eagle wheeling above a steep cliff. The gradient is reasonable, so it's up to you whether you want to attack at full speed or simply cruise up. Do step off the bike at Penhas da Saude at 4,900 feet (1,500 m)—the only winter sports resort in Portugal—to taste the local sheep's cheese. Once over the top, you'll glide down the west slope, amid the most wonderful colors, toward Viseu. Serra da Estrela is a modest place, but the road over it is one of the most beautiful in Europe to cycle.

Le Mur, a Belgian institution

Belgium may be mostly flat, but it has a number of hills so treacherous that their access roads have been dubbed "walls" *(muurs/murs* in Flemish/French). Not far from the cobbled Koppenberg, you'll find the Muur van Geraardsbergen, with its beveled cobbles and a gradient of 19%. By the river Meuse is the Mur de Huy and its 26% bend close at the top. Southeast of Liège, close to the Spa-Francorchamps motor-racing circuit, is the Côte de Stockeu with its 10 to 15% gradient at more than 6,500 feet (2,000 m). To ride any of these is to follow in the traces of the champions of the greatest Classics … though perhaps a little slower.

THE KOPPENBERG, A CONCENTRATION OF EFFORT

213 feet
(60 m)
altitude gain

2,000 feet
(600 m)
of climbing

11.6%
average gradient

22%
maximum gradient

Paved with bad intentions *Koppenberg, Belgium*

We're in Belgium, right in the middle of a triangle formed by Ghent, Lille, and Brussels. At Melden, you turn off the billiard-table smoothness of the N8—which runs alongside the Scheldt River by the appositely named Café Koppenberg—and follow the sign to Zulzeke, then to Koppenberg, as you pedal onto Rue Steengat. Here is where the "horror" begins. It's pretty short, but few seasoned cyclists are able to reach the top of the most fearsome cobbled

peak in the friendly Flemish Ardennes in less than three minutes. The suffering lasts only 2,000 feet (600 m) between two pleasant green embankments. The peloton of the prestigious Tour of Flanders, which is to Flemish people what the Super Bowl is to Americans, tackled this climb for the first time in 1976, when even the larger-than-life Eddy Merckx had to get off the bike. The Koppenberg is torture from the start. Its steepness is unforgiving.

Indeed, it is still the only climb in the world where champions resign themselves to the humiliation of unclipping in order not to topple over, brought to a halt by the gradient. The lopsided cobblestones were re-laid in the 2000s at a cost of $180,000 to the town of Audenarde. The Koppenberg remains a challenge that any cyclist will be proud to have conquered.

Intermittently open

Some of the most legendary photographs in the history of cycling have been taken in the Stelvio Pass: Fausto Coppi, Eddy Merckx, or Bernard Hinault riding between two walls of snow much higher than them. The pass is only open between May and November, and it has frequently featured in the Giro d'Italia. Nature holds sway here. Great humility is therefore required if you wish to tackle the mountain by bike.

1 **8,599 feet (2,621 m) - Gavia** (Lombardy). The Stelvio's "little brother" also has unpaved sections

2 **7,145 feet (2,178 m) - Finestre** (Piedmont). Demanding gradients and a unique backdrop: 32 hairpins through the forest, over a white dirt road, *la sterrata*

3 **7,027 feet (2,142 m) - Blockhaus** (Abruzzo). A long, 17 mile (28 km) climb from Lettomanoppello through the rocky landscape of the Majella

4 **6,076 feet (1,852 m) - Mortirolo** (Lombardy). Complicated climb via Mazzo: only 8 miles (12.5 km) but with four sections at 18%

5 **5,675 feet (1,730 m) - Monte Zoncolan** (Friuli). Very hard via Priola, east slope: 5.5 miles (9 km) but with an average gradient of 13%

Vertiginous *Stelvio Pass, Italy*

The Stelvio is not quite the highest road pass in the Alps. At 9,048 feet (2,758 m), it is 19 feet (6 m) lower than the Iseran in France. It is, however, the one that cyclists fantasize about the most—at least those who adore riding the mountains. The higher you climb, the more vertiginous the snaking road below appears. Make sure that you pick the right slope. The legendary Stelvio, the one with the seemingly infinite hairpins, is the north face,

approached via the Prato, and not from the south via Bormio. We're in Trentino-Alto Adige in the Italian Tyrol. The road was built nearly two hundred years ago to link the Austro-Hungarian Empire with Lombardy, its dependency. The audacious route has changed little since then. There are 60 hairpin bends, 48 of which are numbered in a countdown that encourages—and sometimes discourages—the adventurer. But what a spectacle! Take a coffee break at

Gomagoi, or at the Hotel Franzenshöhe halfway up. If you're in great physical shape, you should be able to climb the Stelvio's 5,905 feet (1,800 m) over 15 miles (24 km) of road in two hours. As you reach the final slopes (at 9%), where the oxygen thins, make sure that you keep looking back down until you reach the summit and the Albergo Tibet. The effect is overwhelming.

Red Sea challenge

The long history of Belgian colonization has
left its traces in Rwanda. The same goes for
Italy's presence in Eritrea, which is 1,800 miles
(3,000 km) to the north, beside the Red Sea. The
first two black Africans to take part in the Tour
de France in 2015—Daniel Teklehaimanot and
Merhawi Kudus—were Eritrean. Their training
ground around Asmara—the capital which lies at
an altitude of 7,800 feet (2,400 m)—is wonderfully
challenging.

WORTHY OF A TOUR DE FRANCE STAGE
Eighty miles (125 km) from Muhanga to Musanze,
through the equatorial forest and the high mountains

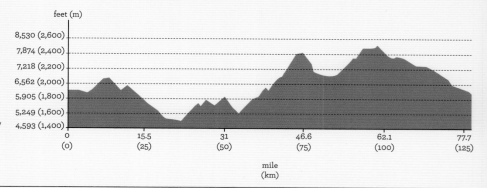

feet (m)

8,530 (2,600)
7,874 (2,400)
7,218 (2,200)
6,562 (2,000)
5,905 (1,800)
5,249 (1,600)
4,593 (1,400)

0   15.5   31   46.6   62.1   77.7
(0)   (25)   (50)   (75)   (100)   (125)

mile
(km)

Ride with the new Colombians *Volcano Route, Rwanda*

Rwanda ended the twentieth century amid genocidal horror. The "land of a thousand hills" is in the process of rebuilding itself, with cycling making a modest contribution. Up on the high plains, you can see a phenomenon similar to the Colombian boom of the 1980s. An American pioneer, Jonathan Boyer, has been working there for years. Young talents have started to come through. The queen stage of the Tour of Rwanda takes the national road

11 to Musanze at the edge of the Volcanoes National Park in the northwest of the country, close to the Congolese border. It is worthy of the finest Alpine routes. Start from Muhanga, 25 miles (40 km) from the capital, Kigali, and already at 6,000 feet (1,800 m), for a lovely 60-mile (100 km) ride up hills, down valleys, and through equatorial forests. As you head toward Mukamira, then Mukingo, you climb two mountain passes at 8,000 feet

(2,500 m). Mount Karisimbi, the highest volcano in the range (14,786 feet/4,507 m), dominates the horizon. Its luxuriant slopes are home to the last wild gorillas in the African Great Lakes region. With the temperature cooled by the altitude, a ride through the Rwandan mountains in July, when everyone in Europe is focused on the Tour de France, is a beautiful homage to this magnificent country.

Cycling and the townships

THE INDIAN, THEN THE ATLANTIC
The most beautiful ocean views on the route of the Cape Town Cycle Tour

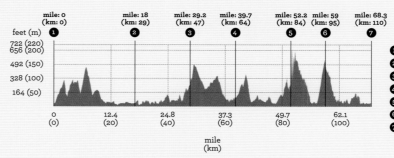

| | mile: 0 (km: 0) | mile: 18 (km: 29) | mile: 29.2 (km: 47) | mile: 39.7 (km: 64) | mile: 52.2 (km: 84) | mile: 59 (km: 95) | mile: 68.3 (km: 110) |

feet (m)
722 (220)
656 (200)
492 (150)
328 (100)
164 (50)

0 (0) 12.4 (20) 24.8 (40) 37.3 (60) 49.7 (80) 62.1 (100)

mile
(km)

1 Start at the Cape
2 Kalk Bay
3 Smitswinkel
4 Misty Cliffs
5 Chapman's Peak
6 Suikerbossie
7 Finish at the Cap

From one ocean to another *Cape Peninsula, South Africa*

South Africans like to pedal out of the cities, across the savannah, and along the ocean. The Cape of Good Hope marks the point where the Atlantic meets the Indian Ocean. The peninsula leading to it is wonderfully suited to cycling. Roadies are quite spoiled here. So forget the much-hyped, though certainly seductive, wine route and instead pedal toward some of the most spectacular ocean views that you will ever see. The route to follow is that of the 60-mile (100 km) Cape Town Cycle Tour, a mass event that celebrates its fortieth year in 2018. As many as 35,000 cyclists ride past the beautiful beaches of the Indian Ocean before turning west toward those of the Atlantic. The corniche of Chapman's Peak—a sand-colored cliff plunging straight into the ocean—offers 5.5 miles (9 km) of the kind of climbing about which one dreams. It is, without a doubt, one of the most beautiful coastal roads in the world. Take note: if you make the return trip to Cape Town in less than three hours, you'll earn the respect of the regulars at the fashionable cycling-orientated coffee shop The Handle Bar.

Al Qudra: the desert road

The Al Qudra road is the pride of the Emirates because it enables Dubaians to escape from their "Manhattan of the Middle East." An 11-mile (18 km) two-way stretch leaves Dubai southward until it meets a 30-mile (50 km) loop that is virtually flat and smoothly surfaced with shaded rest areas. This is right out in the desert, where you can see oryxes (gazelles of the sands) between the dunes. As for the sunrise over Al Qudra, it is quite simply magnificent.

Duration
1 to 2h

Distance
6.7 miles (10.8 km)

Difficulty
very high

Gradient
average: 6.6%
maximum: 11%

WORTHY OF SOME EUROPEAN CLIMBS
Tackling the Jebel Hafeet requires the same humility and total commitment as many alpine passes

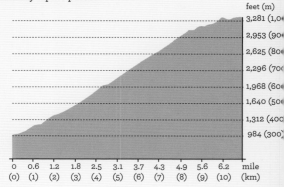

	feet (m)
	3,281 (1,0
	2,953 (90
	2,625 (80
	2,296 (700
	1,968 (600
	1,640 (500
	1,312 (400
	984 (300

0	0.6	1.2	1.8	2.5	3.1	3.7	4.3	4.9	5.6	6.2	mile
(0)	(1)	(2)	(3)	(4)	(5)	(6)	(7)	(8)	(9)	(10)	(km)

A climb from the *Arabian Nights* *Jebel Hafeet, Abu Dhabi*

Europeans and Americans light their ski runs. It would not be very ecologically responsible for them to do the same for famous cycling climbs. The Gulf States are less concerned. In the 1980s, Abu Dhabi built a road up the slopes of Jebel Hafeet (literally, "empty mountain"), which has hundreds of caves and stands on the border with Oman. Then they installed lighting from top to bottom, like a football stadium. Summer night climbs of Jebel Hafeet

have thus become an option for the local cyclists. By day, forget it. Temperatures at the foot of the climb can reach 120°F (50°C) under the searing sun, the air is stifling, and any prolonged effort is impossible. The Jebel Hafeet Mountain Road has three lanes—two for ascending, and one for descending, which is shared with cars—and it snakes through 60 hairpins. It is also something of an optical illusion, which is to say that its

unusual width suggests an easier climb than in reality. There's no illusion as far as your thighs and lungs are concerned, for it maintains an average gradient of 6.6% for the duration of its 7 miles (11 km) until the road tops out at 3,362 feet (1,025 m). But it's worth the effort. The terrace of the Mercure hotel at the summit offers a vision that could have come straight from the Arabian Nights—the thousands of twinkling lights of the city of Al Ain.

Assault on Mount Fuji

Majestic Mount Fuji lies 60 miles (100 km) from Tokyo. More than a symbol of Japan, Mount Fuji also fascinates cyclists. Every June, the Fuji Hill Climb attracts nearly 10,000 competitors. It finishes at the 5th Station at an altitude of 7,503 feet (2,287 m). Beyond, the road is not paved, and soon breaks into trails. It's tough to reach Fuji's summit at 12,389 feet (3,776 m) by mountain bike because there are long sections where you have to shoulder it. The descents, however, are fast and exhilarating.

THE KEIRIN, A CURIOUS INDUSTRY
Developed in Japan in 1948, the keirin sees punters bet on track cyclists as if they were horses

5
billion dollars
The annual total of bets on keirin

9
riders at the start,
obliged to reveal their tactics to the gamblers beforehand

47
velodromes
in Japan have around 20 three-day keirin competitions.

100
yen
($1) is the price of admission

2,545
cyclists
lived off keirin in 2015

2012
the year women were allowed to compete in keirin again

To the sound of the drums *Sado Island, Japan*

Japanese roads are far from being the preserve of cyclists. Once you leave the urban areas, you often have to contend with narrow roads and very heavy traffic, that's on the left. Why not take the ferry from Niigata to Sado Island, a three-hour crossing? Sado Island has a similar surface area to Tahiti and an interesting history. For a long time, it served as a place of banishment for those incurring the emperor's displeasure. In the seventeenth century, gold was found,

and a large mining industry developed there, with the last mine closing in 1989. Today, there are only 60,000 inhabitants. It's a peaceful place. The island is symmetrically shaped and comprises two mountain ranges: Osado (the northern part) and Kosado (the southern part) with a central plain (Kuninaka) that runs between two superb bays, Ryotsu and Mano. The main road traverses the plain and is barely 30 miles (50 km) long. A hybrid bike, such as a gravel, is perfect

for Sado because you can take advantage of the wide, smooth dirt tracks. To the north stretches the sublime Sea of Japan behind Mount Kinpoku, which rises to 3,845 feet (1,172 m). The southern part of Sado offers coastal roads with stunning views and is accessible to all. The oysters from the saltwater Lake Kamo are very tasty, while the displays of traditional taiko drumming in many of the villages are a delight.

How long until a Chinese champion?

In Europe, it's long been thought that extensive daily use of bicycles in China would facilitate the blooming of sporting talent. These days, the concern is rather to get citizens cycling for their well-being. Performance-wise, any success is at the velodrome. The first Chinese rider to compete in the Tour de France was Cheng Li in 2014. He finished last, six hours behind the Yellow Jersey. The Tour of China, established in 1995, receives little media coverage.

70 MILES AROUND DIANCHI LAKE
The Granfondo China endurance race takes place amid the splendors of Yunnan. The first of five itineraries of the race follows the shores of Dianchi Lake, having started out from Kunming. The minimum permitted speed is 11 mph (18 km/h).

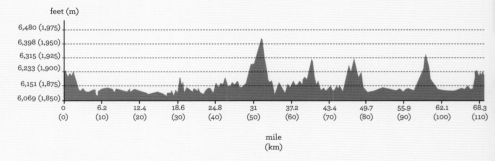

feet (m)

| 6,480 (1,975) |
| 6,398 (1,950) |
| 6,315 (1,925) |
| 6,233 (1,900) |
| 6,151 (1,875) |
| 6,069 (1,850) |

0 (0) — 6.2 (10) — 12.4 (20) — 18.6 (30) — 24.8 (40) — 31 (50) — 37.2 (60) — 43.4 (70) — 49.7 (80) — 55.9 (90) — 62.1 (100) — 68.3 (110)

mile (km)

From the Yangtze to Shangri-La
Yunnan Province, China

Shangri-La was an imaginary place created by the British author James Hilton for his famous novel *Lost Horizon*. With the aim of boosting tourism, it is now also the name of a new town that has smothered the Tibetan charms of the ancestral Zhongdian. We are in the south of China on the edge of the Himalayas. The force of those peaks, the depth of the sky, and the clearness of the light make you think that cycling is simply

not possible over there to the east, the land of trekking. But in Yunnan, which is as large as Germany and where the Yangtze river starts to swell, pretty much everything can be pedaled. Bear in mind the long distances and ensure that you have some logistical support. You're constantly above 6,500 feet (2,000 m) here, so you'll certainly put your body to the test. If you take the Lijiang road, it's well worth making a stop at Tiger Leaping Gorge at the

foot of Mount Yulong, which rises to 18,360 feet (5,596 m). It's paradise. Then leave Lijiang for Panzhihua via a spectacular road with amazing views. Next, head straight south via Kunming, before cycling through the terraced rice paddies of Yuanyang. Or else focus on Xishuangbanna, lower down and closer to the Mekong, between Laos and Burma. In this more tropical climate, reward yourself after a day in the saddle with some chilled coconut milk.

Ave Maria!

The large island of Tasmania is surrounded by a thousand other smaller islands and islets. At Triabunna, just up the coast from Orford, you can rent a mountain bike then take the boat over to Maria Island (where cars are forbidden) to spend the day there. Just make sure you bring everything that you need with you because there aren't any shops. You'll find fabulous beaches, cliffs painted by Aboriginals 10,000 years ago, wombats, wallabies, and kangaroos. It's an extraordinary day out.

TASMANIA, A HUGE NATURE RESERVE

3
inhabitants per
square mile

150 miles
(240 km)
from the Australian
coast to Tasmania

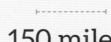

33%
of its surface is
designated as a
nature reserve or
national park

5,305 feet
(1,617 m)
top of the highest
peak, Mount Ossa

Surprising Tasmania *From Orford to St. Helens, Australia*

Ever since one of their own—Cadel Evans—won the Tour de France in 2011, cycling's place in the already strong Australian sports culture has been assured. Some routes are legendary, such as the Great Ocean Road west of Melbourne, or the sumptuous Lions Road between Sydney and Brisbane. But from January to March (which is summertime there), you can also try something a little different that's only an hour and a half's

flight south of Melbourne. Tasmania is roughly the size of Ireland, but it has only half a million inhabitants. Outside of the Hobart area—where you should, of course, climb Pinnacle Road leading to Mount Wellington (4,170 feet/1,271 m)—the highways are quiet and welcoming. The road along the east coast beside the Indian Ocean, from Orford to St. Helens, is a must: 125 miles (200 km) over a couple of intense, spectacular days,

heading where the fancy takes you with no insurmountable difficulty. From Triabunna to Coles Bay, to Bicheno to Scamander, each place seems like paradise. To the right, you'll find an undulating coast with capes, bays, cliffs, and beaches that are ideal for surfing. To the left, you'll see nature reserves and parks, waterfalls, and rivers, as well as famous vineyards that should be paid due homage when you finish.

Mountain bike manufacturers

In 1987, three friends from Chicago—Scott, Ray, and Sam—founded Sram, a bicycle component manufacturer that has become the sole challenger to the Japanese giant, Shimano. They anticipated the coming mountain bike explosion and made a fortune with the grip shift, a technological innovation that allows you to change gear simply by twisting the handlebar grip. It's fair to say that Campagnolo—the somewhat traditional Italian firm that was formerly the market leader—has lost its grip.

SIX GOLDEN DESTINATIONS
Six places—in addition to Sun Valley—that nurtured mountain biking in the United States

❶ **Bend**, Oregon
❷ **Downieville**, California
❸ **Crested Butte**, Colorado
❹ **Blue Ridge**, North Carolina

❺ **Harrisonburg**, Virginia
❻ **East Burke**, Vermont

The conquest of the West *Sun Valley, United States*

Rising above Sun Valley are 14 peaks that form part of the Rockies; all are more than 9,800 feet (3,000 m) high. They are called the Pioneer Mountains in homage to those who forged the history of modern America. Sun Valley was once a forgotten corner of Idaho, where there was nothing but a small silver mine. A trip to Europe persuaded the directors of the Union Pacific Railroad that winter sports would attract a new public to the west. And so it was

that, in the 1930s, Sun Valley became the first ski resort in the United States. The world's first chairlifts were installed here, and there is now a vast network of mechanical lifts open to mountain bikers. A $39 day pass or a $359 year pass provides access to 435 miles (700 km) of marvelous, marked trails. The resort sits at 5,945 feet (1,812 m), and there's an irresistible urge to go even higher and enjoy extraordinary views across the mountainscape, as

well as exciting downhill runs through the pines and mountain pastures, dropping 3,000 feet (1,000 m). The neighboring resorts, Ketchum and Hailey, are just as generous in their offerings. But at the end of the day, it's back to Sun Valley and its 1,400 inhabitants, including Clint Eastwood, for a well-earned drink at the Power House, which is considered to be the best bike and beer pub in the world by its regulars.

Race to the poles

Global warming will get the better of those seeking to conquer the poles. The Arctic sea ice has already receded too much. It is no longer a realistic proposition to head out by bike over the ice from Nunavut at the tip of Canada. In Antarctica, a few explorers have reached the South Pole since 2012 using a combination of fat bike and sled. They include the American Erik Larsen, the Spaniard Juan Menendez Granado—also know as "Juan Sin Miedo" (No Fear Juan)—and two young British women, Helen Skelton and Maria Leijerstam.

SIX DAYS OF SAVAGE BEAUTY
Starting from Anchorage, ride out on a magnificent tour of the Chugach Mountains

● **Day 1 :** Anchorage > Wasilla, (45 miles /70 km)
● **Day 2 :** Wasilla > Sheep Mountain Lodge (55 miles/90 km)
● **Day 3 :** Sheep Mountain Lodge > Copper Center (75 miles/120 km)
● **Day 4 :** Copper Center > Valdez (100 miles/160 km)
● **Day 5 :** Valdez > Whittier, three-hour ferry crossing of Prince William Sound (icebergs probable), (90 miles/145 km)
● **Day 6 :** Whittier > Anchorage (60 miles/ 100 km)

Duration
5 to 7 days

Distance
425 miles
(685 km)

Difficulty
average

Gear
road bike and
winter clothing

Surprises in Anchorage *Alaska, United States*

Jack London loved cycling, but only did a little of it in Alaska. London described the northernmost American state, which is three times the size of France yet has barely 700,000 inhabitants, as "a country where whisky freezes solid and may be used as a paperweight for a large part of the year." It's hard to imagine this territory—stuck between the Bering Sea and the Arctic Ocean—as a cycling destination because it's a land of glaciers,

volcanoes, moonscape valleys, and grizzlies; teeming with mosquitoes; and the scene of summer wildfires caused by lightning. Yet, you only have to leave Anchorage to realize what a superb playground it is. Look east, where the sun rises above the Chugach Mountains. At their foot is the eponymous national park, the second-largest forest in the United States—a wild territory that is very easy to access. The chairlifts of Alyeska

Resort have a view over the taiga. On the other side, along Cook Inlet, Kincaid Park offers 45 miles (70 km) of forest and coastal trails, most of them accessible to everyone. June to September is the best cycling season, when the temperature rises above 40°F (5°C). For the rest of the year, a fatbike and winter gear are essential.

Gary Fisher and his buddies

There is no single inventor of the mountain bike, but the mustachioed Gary Fisher is often mentioned. Fisher was one of the guys who liked to tinker with old Schwinns at the Tamalpais Cycling Club. But his buddies, Joe Breeze, Charlie Kelly, and Tom Ritchey—the latter now a respected bicycle frame builder—all made just as much of a contribution. Nobody, however, has ever contested the birthplace of the mountain bike as anywhere but Mount Tamalpais.

FORTY YEARS OF MOUNTAIN BIKING

1979
Tom Ritchey creates the Mountain Bikes brand

1981
Specialized launches its first Stumpjumper, a now legendary model

1984
The first mountain bike event in Europe, the Roc d'Azur, has seven entrants

1989
The first hydraulic suspension fork makes its appearance

1994
The first brake discs for bicycles go on sale

2016
One in four bikes sold in the United States is a mountain bike, out of a total 16 million units a year

Where the mountain bike was born

Mount Tamalpais, United States

There are two reasons to climb to the top of Mount Tamalpais, the highest peak in the Marin Hills at 2,571 feet (785 m). The first is for the view over the Pacific Ocean and the city of San Francisco, which is 12 miles (20 km) to the south. The second is because it is the birthplace of the mountain bike. Coming here is like a pilgrimage. It was here in the pine woods of Marin County, along a 2.5-mile (4 km) firebreak, that the first mountain bike prototypes were tested in the 1970s, in friendly races. Hippie culture saw some former roadies converted to the cause; they found it "cool" to customize old Schwinn cruisers. The first models were pretty rudimentary: weighing more than 45 pounds (20 kg), single speed— equivalent to the old 52 x 14 much loved by Jacques Anquetil—with back pedal brakes that were so unsuited to such extreme usage that the grease would start to smoke during long descents. The pioneers were obliged to disassemble the brakes and repack the grease after each run, hence the nickname that they gave their competitions: Repack Races. The gentle slope of the original Tamalpais trail makes you smile today. Still, those guys managed to reach top speeds of more than 45 mph. This is where it all began.

Do you speak Québécois?

From Montreal to Mont-Sainte-Anne, French-speaking Canadians have their own cycling vocabulary, which is a mix of English and French. A mountain bike is a *vélo de montagne* (a literal translation), while a hybrid bike for tooling around town is a *bécyk*. If it rains, you must *met la bâche* ("tarp up"). After a race, you give an *entrevue*, not an "interview." But if you want to prevent your bike from getting stolen, or repair a puncture, you simply use a "lock" or a "patch."

SIX CANADIAN ESSENTIALS
Comox Valley may have a reputation as the place to go mountain biking in Canada, but there are alternatives

❶ **Vancouver Island**, British Columbia
❷ **Whistler**, British Columbia
❸ **Mont-Sainte-Anne**, Québec

❹ **Jasper National Park**, Alberta
❺ **Hardwood Hills**, Ontario
❻ **Bromont**, Québec

The keys to paradise *Vancouver Island, Canada*

The Canada of vast expanses and mountainous terrain is a natural treasure trove for bicycling enthusiasts. Indeed, mountain biking is perhaps even more popular here than in the United States. Way out west is an island, the largest on the entire Pacific coast, more than 250 miles (400 km) long by 50 miles (80 km) wide. It bears the name of the large and beautiful city across the water on the mainland: Vancouver. Between its highest point, the Golden Hinde at

7,201 feet (2,195 m), and the Strait of Georgia lies Comox Valley, which is paradise on Earth for mountain bikers. With a little seismic help, the rainfall and the temperate forest climate have fashioned an original and surprising landscape that is well-suited to cross-country biking and trekking. You'll never be bored here among the cedars, Douglas firs, and mountain lakes, even if you're not a champion cyclist. Summer also brings a host of festivals

to enjoy on beautiful Vancouver Island, with a glass of Cowichan Valley white wine in your hand.

Across Central America

It's an epic ride organized by the French Bicycle
Touring Federation, lasting three months and taking
in eight countries—Mexico, Belize, Guatemala, El
Salvador, Honduras, Nicaragua, Costa Rica, and
Panama—at an average rate of 50 miles (80 km) a
day. There are all sorts of routes, many of them quite
mountainous. It's a wonderful way of combining
exercise and culture.

LA VUELTA DEL LAGO ARENAL
A mountain bike race open to men, women, and children

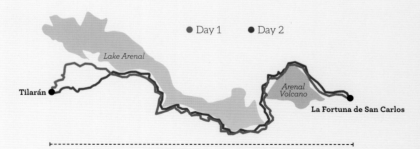

● Day 1   ● Day 2

Lake Arenal

Tilarán

*Arenal
Volcano*

La Fortuna de San Carlos

90 miles (145 km), there and back

Pleasures of the Pura Vida *Lake Arenal, Costa Rica*

If there is one country where you can savor all of the ingredients of a perfect cross-country adventure, it is Costa Rica, the green jewel of Central America. The national slogan is Pura vida! (literally, "pure life," but also suggestive of a carefree, relaxed, and optimistic perspective). There are quiet roads, bumpy trails, and breathtaking views, making for some top-notch mountain-biking sites. At the instigation of a president who declared "peace with nature," Costa Rica has become a pioneer of ecotourism and a world leader in biodiversity protection. It's a pleasure to tackle the slopes of volcanoes, to gaze out over turquoise-colored lakes, to traverse a luxuriant jungle, and to ride along heavenly Pacific beaches. Lake Arenal, which lies just northwest of the volcano of the same name, has a surface area of 35 square miles (85 km²), and is 60 miles (100 km) from the capital, San José.

This body of water is surrounded by verdant hills with a vibrant fauna that includes hummingbirds, toucans, howler monkeys, and jaguars. If you're after technical, physically demanding biking, combined with a sense of adventure, Lake Arenal is ideal, particularly because it is an active volcano.

Good vibes at the Fat Tyre Festival

Perhaps the "coolest" mountain-biking event is the one held in Jamaica every February. The Fat Tyre Festival offers a week of climbs and descents in the hills of Saint Mary Parish, in northeast Jamaica, the cradle of dancehall reggae. With its sporty yet relaxed atmosphere, the festival is a unique way to discover the culture of the island. Even the event's official beer—Red Stripe, brewed in the capital—has a light, festive taste.

FASTER THAN USAIN BOLT!
A theoretical match between the Jamaican athlete and a champion cyclist

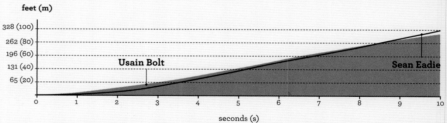

Biomechanics expert Jim Martin has concluded that, based on Bolt's 100-meter world record run of 9.58 set in Berlin in 2009, the world champion track cyclist Sean Eadie would have caught Usain Bolt at 90 meters, despite being slower to start with his bike, and that he would have beaten Bolt by 16 hundredths of a second. (Source: *Outside Magazine*, June 2010)

Reggae ride *Blue Mountains, Jamaica*

Jamaica may be focused on seaside tourism, but it does have other treasures in store. The island has all the elements that make for some extraordinary cross-country rides. The Blue Mountains cover the eastern third of the island are a UNESCO World Heritage Site. Blue Mountain Peak is the highest point in Jamaica and one of the highest mountains in the Caribbean at 7,402 feet (2,256 m). From the summit, you can see the Cuban coast 125 miles (200 km) away when the weather is fine. For more than a century, its slopes provided hideouts for escaped slaves. These days, some of the best and most expensive coffee in the world is grown here. Located only an hour from Kingston, the luxuriant forest offers numerous itineraries, with opportunities to meet friendly villagers and ride through coffee and banana plantations. The highly varied terrain (mud, earth, and rock) is widely accessible and provides spectacular views from north to south, and from Buff Bay to Kingston. When the day's cycling is done, you can find an embarrassing choice of refreshing waterfalls and relaxing beaches—to enjoy to a reggae beat, of course!

In the jungle of Cancún

People don't generally come to Cancún, which is considered the flower of the Mexican tourist industry on the Caribbean Sea, to go cycling. Yet you can easily spend a couple of fun days mountain biking here. The Punta Venado bike park, which is close to Playa del Carmen, offers miles of marked trails through the jungle, where you can see ruins of Mayan architecture. But watch out, Cancún means "nest of snakes" in Mayan.

COPPER CANYON (BARRANCA DEL COBRE)
Copper Canyon comprises six gorges deeper than the Grand Canyon in Arizona (maximum 4,900 feet/1,500 m).

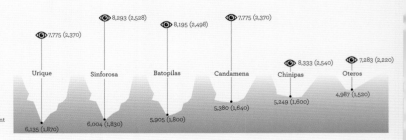

👁 7,775 (2,370)

👁 8,293 (2,528)

👁 8,195 (2,498)

👁 7,775 (2,370)

👁 8,333 (2,540)

👁 7,283 (2,220)

Urique

Sinforosa

Batopilas

Candamena

Chinipas

Oteros

4,987 (1,520)

👁 Height of the viewpoint

• Depth

6,135 (1,870)

6,004 (1,830)

5,905 (1,800)

5,380 (1,640)

5,249 (1,600)

feet (m)

Very grand canyons

Sierra Madre, Chihuahua, Mexico

You have to really want to go there. After a two-and-a-half hour flight from Mexico City, you spend three hours in the Chepe, a train that connects Chihuahua City to the Pacific Ocean, before finishing the journey in an old American school bus. All that for a bike ride? Sure. It's no ordinary bike ride. Barranca del Cobre (Copper Canyon), in the heart of the western Sierra Madre in northwest Mexico, is an unusual place: a string of six amazingly deep canyons covering 40 miles (70 km). Even in the baking spring heat of the high plains—between 6,500 feet (2,000 m) and 8,000 feet (2,500 m)—you'll never tire of these vertiginous panoramas of sliced-up mountains, arid landscapes, forests of oak and pine, and the ever-shifting colors of the rock. The terrain is extraordinary, even if you have to remain prudent. This is where the first scenes of the TV show *Man vs. Wild* were filmed. Numerous narrow, technical trails descend to the rivers, which can only be crossed by a few hanging bridges. Don't miss Basaseachi Falls at 807 feet (246 m) high, or a traditional ceremony held by the Tarahumara indigenous people, the residents of Barranca del Cobre.

The Galápagos, after Darwin

Among the reasons to visit the Galápagos Islands—
which lie in the Pacific Ocean, 600 miles (1,000
km) off the coast of Ecuador—are the giant turtles,
iguanas, sea lions, and the memory of Charles
Darwin's work on evolution. But mountain biking is
another reason, notably on the main island, Isabela.
The jungle trails leading to the Wolf (5,600 feet/1,707
m) and Cerro Azul (5,541 feet/1,689 m) volcanoes
hold their own special attraction. Do ride as a group
and never alone.

FIVE RIDES AROUND QUITO
The Ecuadorian capital, which lies at 9,350 feet (2,850 m), and the surrounding region
have some lovely surprises

❶ **Parque Métropolitano, in the northern neighborhoods
of Quito:** the capital's green lung covers 1,377 acres (557
hectares)

❷ **The Pululahua Geobotanical Reserve (25 miles/40 km from
Quito):** the country's oldest national park

❸ **Imbabura (60 miles/100 km from Quito):** an inactive
volcano that is part of the Andes

❹ **Ambuquí (90 miles /150 km from Quito):** in the Chora
Valley, where there are many sugarcane plantations, as
well as traditional dwellings built from rammed earth

❺ **Cahuasquí (90 miles /150 km from Quito):** start from here,
a small village on a plateau surrounded by gorges, on a ride
through the Andean desert

Lava and ash *Cotopaxi, Ecuador*

The silhouette of Cotopaxi, which is 40 miles (60 km) south of Quito, can be a worrying sight. In 2015, this volcano, whose eruptions have been national disasters, awoke from its slumber. A shower of ash reached the capital, and maximum alert was declared. The slopes of Cotopaxi—19,347 feet (5,897 m) at its summit—are a special place to mountain bike as long as you take the proper precautions, including keeping an eye on the weather forecast, because there can sometimes be thick fog. Cotopaxi can present an austere sight, marked by lava flows and ash, yet it is also inspiring with alpine tundra lower down and snowy slopes farther up, topped by an almost perfect peak that is 2,600 feet (800 m) in diameter. There are two options; neither of which is easy because you're at a high altitude. The most fun is to drive to the top of the 4 x 4 trail at 15,000 feet (4,600 m), then bike down. The descent is neither too steep nor too technical. The other is extreme: conquer Cotopaxi by pedal force alone. Take care, because your heart will soon be beating hard at this altitude, and there will still be nearly 6,500 feet (2,000 m) of climbing in front of you. You'll need hours, alpine style, as if you were in the Himalayas. Some say that Cotopaxi means "shining mountain" in an indigenous language. What's for sure is that it is an exhilarating experience. Just keep your wits about you.

Ushuaia, south of the South

Ushuaia may be the southernmost city in the world, but you can do a good day's cycling in the surrounding area—between December and March, that is, when the maximum temperature is a balmy 50°F (10°C). It's a return trip heading out southeast on the coastal trails that run along Beagle Channel, which separates Tierra del Fuego (Argentina) from Navarino Island (Chile). The wooded hills, rocky landscapes, and Les Eclaireurs Lighthouse are quite sublime in the amazing light here at the end of the world.

ROAD OF THE SEVEN LAKES
From San Martín de los Andes to San Carlos de Bariloche

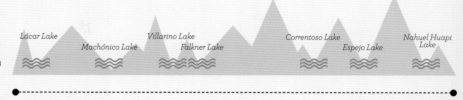

Lácar Lake
Machónico Lake
Villarino Lake
Falkner Lake
Correntoso Lake
Espejo Lake
Nahuel Huapi Lake

San Martín de los Andes   118 miles (190 km)   San Carlos de Bariloche

Switzerland of the gauchos
Bariloche Region, Patagonia, Argentina

The history of San Carlos de Bariloche, situated 995 miles (1,600 km) from Buenos Aires, is a recent one. The town was founded in 1902 and is the oldest winter sports site in South America. It's first official inhabitant was a Swiss man. The influx of foreigners and its tourist ambitions earned it the nickname "Little Switzerland." The surrounding province of Río Negro is quite magnificent—a land of forests, lakes, valleys, and mountains stretching as far as the eye can see. It's like the Andes of the south, but at alpine altitudes. To the west sits the extinct Tronador volcano (11,453 feet/3,554 m). There are some thrilling descents, such as El Condor, on the slopes of the nearby Cerro Catedral (7,890 feet/2,405 m). The Road of the Seven Lakes, to the north of Bariloche, is ideal for both endurance riding and touring—each to their own rhythm. There is much to marvel at: the green waters of the rivers, the tumbling cascades, the extraordinary viewpoints, the narrow paths, and the crystal clear waters of Espejo Lake. The route commences on an undulating asphalt road, with the option of switching onto a more technical trail halfway along. At the end, you'll find an *asado* (selection of grilled meats) and a glass of Malbec. Not quite Switzerland, but no matter.

Snow? Get a fat bike!

Alta Badia is a key destination for fat biking. These contraptions, which boast oversized tires four to five inches wide, have recently become immensely popular. With a relatively low tire pressure, you can travel faster and farther than using snowshoes or even skis. Fat bikes are also effective in sand—so much so that you can now cruise the dunes of the Sahara.

LA SELLA RONDA, A CLASSIC
This extraordinary course, which is facilitated by ski lifts, offers the best of the Dolomites

66 miles
(58 km)
distance

5 to 6
hours

12%
in gondolas

7,874 feet
(2,400 m)
altitude gain in gondolas,
then 3,346 feet (1,020 m)
by bike

Scenic Dolomites *Alta Badia, Italy*

The thrusting limestone peaks of the Dolomites, which often have flat summits, overlook mountain pastures and conifer forests. They look more like something that you would expect to find amid the vastness of the American northwest. But we're in Italy, a good two hours by car and north of Venice. Alta Badia, one of the most popular winter sports resorts in the Dolomites, is paradise for two-wheeled adventurers once winter has passed, with more than 600 miles (1,000 km) of trails for all levels. You can even take your bike on the ski lifts as far as Val Gardena and Cortina d'Ampezzo for even more enjoyment. But it's really around Alta Badia, which has become the European capital of mountain biking, that you'll find the most excitement in the South Tyrol, with demanding climbs and thrilling descents between rocks and vertiginous drops. As long as you're in very good physical shape, you should absolutely attempt one of the two variants of the Sella Ronda, which, at 30 miles (50 km), takes a whole day—one you will never forget. It offers three majestic peaks in view: Boé, Selva, and Pisciadu.

La Mer de Glace by bike!

It's possible to pedal up to Montenvers station, at
an altitude of 6,233 feet (1,900 m), where there's a
spectacular view over the famous glacier in the Mont-
Blanc massif, La Mer de Glace. It's a physical climb
alongside the rack railway, with some tricky portions
where you have to shoulder the bike. The descent via
the narrow Caillets path requires good technical skills.
There is a sublime view from Montenvers over La Mer
de Glace and the peaks of the Grande and Petite
Aiguille du Dru and the Grandes Jorasses.

THE TOP TEN SPOTS IN THE FRENCH ALPS

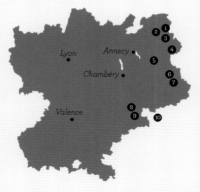

1. Morzine
2. Les Gets
3. Samoëns
4. Chamonix
5. Les Saisies
6. Les Arcs
7. Tignes-Val d'Isère
8. L'Alpe-d'Huez
9. Les Deux Alpes
10. Serre-Chevalier

Mont Blanc is watching you *Chamonix, France*

Chamonix is renowned the world over for mountaineering and top-level skiing. Fans of "real" mountains flock to the foot of Mont Blanc in the thousands, which gives the town a very cosmopolitan feel. Mountain biking very much has its place here. The valleys to the north of Chamonix, toward Switzerland and Martigny, are the starting points for some amazing high-altitude treks, with the most impressive summits at the borders of France, Switzerland, and Italy in your sights. The Col de la Balme trail is very popular, particularly in July and August. At Le Tour, before Vallorcine, you take the Charamillon platter lift with your bike, then you ride as far as the Col des Posettes (6,551 feet/1,997 m), and on toward the Col de la Balme (7,201 feet/2,195 m), which marks the border with Switzerland, though you remain on the French side. The trail from the Posettes to the Balme provides a stunning vista over Mont Blanc. It's very well marked and takes you as far as the pines of the Col des Montets. This four-hour trek (at a good speed) is considered by many to be the most attractive ride in the French mountains.

Bicycle Thieves, nothing changes

Neither Vittorio De Sica, the director, nor Luigi Bartolini, author of the novel that inspired the movie, were Ligurian. Still, why not prepare for an Italian trek by watching *Bicycle Thieves*? In this masterpiece of cinema, a humble billposter has his bicycle stolen and traverses the city looking for it. The movie dates from 1948, but it is just as relevant to cyclists today because nobody wants to get their ride pinched.

LA MARINA, A FANTASTIC LOOP
From scrubland to the creeks of the Riviera

Chapel of San Lorenzino ③
④ Boragni
Grotte Edera ②
⑥
Torre delle Streghe ⑤
Finish at the Julia Augusta Roman road
① Finale Ligure

Duration
5h

Distance
25 miles
(40 km)

Difficulty
high

Height difference
3,559 feet
(1,085 m)

Panorama over the Mediterranean *Finale Ligure, Italy*

Situated halfway between Monaco and Genoa, Finale Ligure would be a quiet seaside resort on the Italian Riveria if it were not for mountain biking. It has become one of the go-to mountain-biking spots in Europe. The terrain has an incredible potential for all types of riding, with some relaxed sections and others that are more technical, promising fast trails and tough climbs. The area is vast: 850 miles (1,370 km) of trails, dotted with small, colorful villages, and pretty sheltered creeks. The Finale Ligure Marina loop includes an incursion into the scrub of the hinterland, with breathtaking panoramas revealing the deep blue of the Mediterranean Sea on the horizon. This 25-mile (40 km) trek makes a change from many of the usual routes around here, which are generally focused on descents. You'll cycle on roads, rocky trails, and through a thick forest before the finish that overlooks the coast. And Liguria is not only for champions; there's also a 16-mile (26 km) cycle path that is perfect for families. When you feel like a break, just take a seat in one of the many gelaterias by the sea, and be soothed by the scent of lemon and hibiscus trees.

Energizing!

Dietrich Mateschitz, the founder of Red Bull—the drink that "gives you wings"—is Austrian. His advertising is based on thrills, and his brand sponsors some of the craziest mountain-biking feats, including terrifying descents, improbable runs, and dizzying jumps. Three hundred people work in Salzburg directing, filming, and editing these extreme performances, which are broadcast free around the world. It is costly marketing, but it pays off.

THE TOP FIVE SPOTS IN THE TYROL
Apart from the Paznaun Valley, here are the most beautiful mountain-biking sites in Austria

1 Nauders
2 Achen Lake (Achensee)

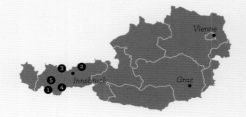

3 Zugspitze
4 Sölden
5 Serfaus-Fiss-Ladis

Sensational Tyrol *Paznaun Valley, Austria*

It's no easier choosing a dream site for mountain biking in the Austrian Tyrol than it is in the French or Swiss Alps: there is a multitude of spots to suit all practices and desires in the western part of the country of Mozart and Schwarzenegger. There was even a two-week Tyrol Mountain Bike Safari covering 435 miles (700 km) created in 2014, from Ischgl in the west to Walchsee in the east, on the other side of Innsbruck. It's a good idea to stay in a guesthouse in the village of Ischgl, located at 4,517 feet (1,377 m). The Paznaun Valley, which commences here, is the perfect distillation of everything you might seek in terms of cross-country pleasure. There is a dense network of ski lifts that are open in summer, hiking trails at more than 6,500 feet (2,000 m), idyllic 360-degree panoramas, and hair-raising descents. Above the high mountain pastures, the sight of glaciers contrasts with the hues of the schist paths and rocks. It's calming. From Ischgl, there's seemingly no end to the wonderfully well-marked trails of the Silvretta Arena, which is a skiing area in winter. In early August, you can test your mettle in the best-known mountain-biking marathon in Europe—the Iron Bike—which covers nearly 50 miles (80 km), with 13,000 feet (4,000 m) of height difference.

Saint-Luc, the Mecca

If you had to pick a single mountain-biking location in this rich canton of Valais, it might be Saint-Luc, a village that is perched between 4,900 feet (1,500 m) and 5,900 feet (1,800 m) in the shadow of Zermatt, a prestigious neighbor. In 2015, Saint-Luc was named the most beautiful mountain-biking site in the whole of the Alps by the British newspaper *The Guardian*. Its trails dry out before those of its neighbors, owing to their exposure to the sun, and its funicular opens in May. Of particular note is its Balcon trail.

VALAIS ALPINE BIKE, A FANTASTIC ENDURO
A legendary course, from Verbier to Sierre (Chandolin), with views of the biggest Swiss peaks over 13,123 feet (4,000 m)

- Verbier > Nendaz (18.5 miles/30 km)
- Nendaz > Saint-Martin (28.5 miles/46 km)
- Saint-Martin > Grimentz via Nax (23.5 miles/38 km)
- Grimentz > Sierre (Chandolin) (17 miles/27 km)

Switzerland
Verbier
Nax
Sierre
Nendaz
Saint-Martin
Grimentz
Verbier

Duration	**Distance**	**Difficulty**	**Height difference**
7 to 10h	87.5 miles (141 km)	high	16,076 feet (4,900 m)

The merry Alps   *Canton of Valais, Switzerland*

Mountain biking is incredibly popular in Switzerland. It's true that, quite apart from the many joys of its topography, two local bicycle manufacturers, Scott and BMC, are among the few to challenge the American and Asian heavyweights in terms of technology. But as soon as the purchase or rental decision has been made, there comes another conundrum: Where to ride? It's no insult to the Grisons (Austria's neighbors) if the Valais, which runs along the Rhône Valley, has a privileged position. Within 60 miles (100 km), there's a succession of sites, each more breathtaking than the last: Émosson and its dam, Verbier, Crans-Montana, Saint-Luc, Zermatt, and so on. At the foot of and on the slopes of the mountains, the villages are sunny and the vineyards promising. Higher up, there are views north over sparkling glaciers; and south, to soaring peaks over 13,000 feet (4,000 m), including the amazing Matterhorn above Zermatt. These magnificent landscapes of high mountain pastures and rocks are wonderful for mountain biking, with hundreds of miles of trails for trekking, enduro, or descending. Come evening, with the bike up on the rack, the Valaisans love to entertain.

Friday bike day in Cairo

Each Friday—the weekly day of rest in Egypt—joggers and cyclists take over Cairo's almost deserted streets. Relieved of those massive traffic jams, the face of the megalopolis changes. Although cycling is still seen as something of a childish activity in Egypt, the movement is growing, thanks to social media. There is still some way to go before it becomes a widespread leisure activity, according to the founder of the Pdal group, which has fueled this enthusiasm.

ODYSSEY IN THE DUNES
An XXL trek through the Western Desert, taking in temples, mummies, springs, oases, and the Nile

- Cairo > Al-Bahariya Oasis, **230 miles** (370 km)
- Al-Bahariya Oasis > Al-Farafra Oasis, **118 miles** (190 km)
- Al-Farafra Oasis > Al-Dakhla Oasis, **205 miles** (330 km)
- Al-Dakhla Oasis > Al-Kharga Oasis, **118 miles** (190 km)
- Al-Kharga Oasis > Luxor, **236 miles** (380 km)

Duration
at least
20 days

Distance
907 miles
(1,460 km)

Difficulty
extreme; a support
vehicle is necessary

Gear
mountain bike,
possibly a fatbike

At the city gates *Wadi Degla, Cairo, Egypt*

Lovers of nature and silence (and mountain biking) will find what they're looking for in an unexpected place, just a few miles from the center of the sprawling city of Cairo. Leave behind the tumult of the Egyptian capital and the droves of tourists at the archaeological sites, and you'll enter another world. South of the city, barely 6 miles (10 km) from the pyramids of Giza, lies Wadi Degla, one of the gateways to the Sahara and a nature reserve. As long as you make sure to set out at the right time of day to avoid the crushing heat, and you carry plenty of extra water, it's a discovery to die for. The landscape evokes certain parts of the American West with its steep paths, rocky outcrops, and space to breathe. You'll see hardly anyone else out here, except some occasional hikers, and cars driving along the valley floor. The owls and gazelles will remind you that you're really at the edge of the desert.

It's an easily accessible trek, and the varied terrain allows for a lovely break in the middle of one of the cradles of humanity.

Mégavalanche = mega thrills

In northwest Réunion, across the island from the active Piton de la Fournaise volcano, the slopes of Maïdo have been the stage for the Mégavalanche—the queen of marathon descents—which has been held every December since 1995. Hundreds of riders from all over the world tear down the now legendary 15-mile (25 km) route to the Plage des Brisants at Saint-Gilles, a descent of 7,200 feet (2,200 m). The event's creator, George Edwards, has successfully transported the concept to France, notably at Alpe-d'Huez.

A TROUBLE-FREE DESCENT
Some mountain-biking descending tips for the less experienced

Bike
disc brakes and front forks with suspension

Gear
elbow pads, knee pads, gloves, and a helmet are essential

Suppleness
arms and legs relaxed and slightly bent

Vigilance
look where you're going in order to anticipate obstacles

Lava story · *Réunion Island, France*

In April 2007, the Piton de la Fournaise volcano, at 8,635 feet (2,631 m), rumbled like never before. Over the course of a month, an eruption that was bigger than any experienced on the island since man first settled there four centuries ago occurred. It reconfigured the landscape. The lava flows forced the authorities to redirect the coastal road at the foot of the volcano. Life returned to normal, as did mountain biking, which had long been practiced on the volcano's slopes—one of the most active on Earth—and across this island in the Indian Ocean, which is recognized as a mountain-biking paradise. Right at the top, on the edge of the Falaise de l'Enclos, which surrounds the volcano's crater, all you can see on the horizon is the Indian Ocean wherever you turn. Réunion Island is a lush tropical garden, but up here, the landscape is stone and rock, all reds and browns. You should wear elbow and knee pads if you're planning a sporty descent; a fall on solidified lava can be painful. Halfway down, the vegetation starts to thicken. As you reach the bottom, you will feel the adrenaline dissipate as you cruise through guava trees and vanilla plantations. It's warm, humid, and very pleasant—so much so that it can be hard to imagine the fear of the islanders in that spring of 2007.

Fatbike: after the snow, the desert

If you prefer peaceful rides to thrills and spills, you'll find many agencies in Namibia offering guided safaris by fatbike. This mountain bike, fitted with extra-wide tires, will take you from the Namib Desert to the Skeleton Coast, to climb dunes and follow trails across the infinite expanses of sand as far as the Atlantic Coast. There can be few better ways to experience the magic of Namibia.

8
inhabitants
per square mile

5
neighboring
countries

104°F
(40°C) temperature
difference between day
and night in the desert, from
December to February

80
million
years: estimated age
of the Namib Desert

Desert thrills *Spitzkoppe, Namibia*

The Spitzkoppe is not only popular with climbers, but also offers excitement to cyclists. This group of granite peaks in the Namib Desert in southwest Africa rises about 2,300 feet (700 m) above the surrounding plain—one of the hottest on the face of the planet—which itself lies at 3,200 feet (1,000 m) above sea level. The sight is made all the more impressive by the fact that the terrain around the Spitzkoppe is quite flat. You have to climb it with your bike

on your back before making a dizzying descent over the rock or along extremely narrow paths. The "Matterhorn of Namibia" is one of the most extreme spots sought out by daredevils from around the world. Although the age-old rock provides a huge amount of grip, you still need nerves of steel. Not everyone is capable of undertaking this gravity-defying challenge in such a remote place, where the only living beings you're likely

to meet are hyraxes (small mammals that look like marmots), herds of springbok, or cobras. Don't forget to bring enough water. If you throw in the towel, you can still explore the exceptional artwork of the San people, who are indigenous to this part of southern Africa.

In Russian Lapland

Another fabulous option for mountain bikers is a trek across the Kola Peninsula (in summer of course!) from the city of Murmansk, which is situated 125 miles (200 km) from the Finnish border. Lying between the Barents Sea and the White Sea, Russian Lapland has much to offer, including polar forest, herds of reindeer, *kota* (a dwelling similar to a teepee), and hot berry juices. The routes are accessible to all levels of experience, and they lie between 650 feet (200 m) and 1,650 feet (500 m) in altitude.

A FEEL FOR KAMCHATKA

North of Japan, there is a marvelous peninsula more than 600 miles (1,000 km) long, which is perfect for mountain bikers. Fly to Petropavlovsk-Kamchatsky, then hire a local guide to take you to Klyuchi.

500 miles
(800 km) distance

2
weeks

When
July and August

Return
by truck

The colors of the Urals *Magnitogorsk, Russia*

Magnitogorsk was once a closed city—off-limits to foreigners—and the Soviet steel capital. During the Cold War, it was where the USSR manufactured half of its battle tanks. The post-Soviet era has seen the city of 420,000 inhabitants, which is located 60 miles (100 km) from the border with Kazakhstan and 870 miles (1,400 km) from Moscow, undertake a radical rebranding as "the place where Europe and Asia meet." This official slogan is quite accurate, because Magnitogorsk straddles the Ural River, which separates the two continents. Its citizens cross from one continent to the other to go to work or do their shopping. On the way, they pass many bikers who are helmeted and kitted out, en route for the nearby ski resorts of Bannoye Lake and Abzakovo, which are less than an hour's drive away. Once the snow has melted, they become superb mountain-biking destinations until autumn's vibrant colors start to fade. The landscape is covered with forests of birch and pine. Here, south of the Ural Mountains, the terrain is gently undulating, with plains stretching as far as the eye can see. The highest point in the region is Bashmak at 3,090 feet (942 m). It's perfect for both tranquil rides and fast descents.

Keep to the left!

Despite its very high humidity, Hong Kong has plenty of road cyclists. Dedicated cycle lanes beside the water lead out of the denser urban areas. There are hillier routes toward Victoria Peak on Hong Kong Island, or Sai Kung West Country Park in the New Territories. Remember to ride on the left—a leftover from the days of British rule—although the rest of China drives on the right.

THE BEST MOUNTAIN-BIKING ROUTES IN HONG KONG

+ sporty

Name: Chi Ma Wan trail, Lantau Island

Distance: 6 to 11 miles (10 to 18 km)

Info: rocky slopes, carry bike on some sections

+ technical

Name: Lamma Island

Distance: 9 miles (15 km)

Info: physically and technically hard

+ popular

Name: Tai Mo Shan, in the north of the New Territories

Distance: 2.5 miles (4 km)

Info: technical descent

+ family

Name: Olympic Trail, Lantau Island

Distance: 7.5 miles (12 km)

Info: moderate difficulty

+ panoramic

Name: Dragon's Back, Hong Kong Island

Distance: 4.5 miles (7 km)

Expat playground *Lantau Island, Hong Kong*

The image of Hong Kong is one of clichés: the skyscrapers of the world's third financial center, the memory of Bruce Lee, and the attraction of neighboring Macau. If you hadn't tried it yourself, you would never think to associate mountain biking with the former British colony that was returned to the People's Republic of China in 1997. It is, however, a fact: this territory, which is comparable to Luxembourg in size, is one of the most attractive mountain-biking destinations that exists. The reason is simple: the sprawl of the impressive megacity was halted at the foot of the densely wooded hills (which characterize the region) for fear of triggering landslides. In the 1990s, the active communities of expats— mainly English-speaking—realized that these hills, which remain perfectly dry in winter, would be perfect for mountain biking. The locals soon followed, and now the mountain bike reigns supreme in the hills and mountains of the islands of Hong Kong, Lamma, Lantau, and the New Territories farther north. The very popular Chi Ma Wan trail on Lantau Island climbs the slopes of Lantau Peak, which rises to 3,064 feet (934 m). It's the perfect place to combine exercise with meditative contemplation.

Delightful four-cross

The 2014 Winter Olympics in Sochi saw three Frenchmen share the ski cross podium, which was a first. Ski cross is a simple yet spectacular racing event. Four competitors race together down a steep, bumpy, winding course that is 2,000 feet (600 m) long. The winner is the first to cross the line. The formula has been copied by mountain biking as "four-cross," although it has had some difficulty finding its legitimacy ever since it was removed from the World Championships program in 2012. It's a shame, because it's as much fun on bikes as it is on skis.

SIX SPOTS AROUND THE BLACK SEA
The most spectacular mountain-biking destinations of each country on the Black Sea

1 Russia > Sochi
2 Georgia > Kazbek
3 Turkey > Cappadocia chimneys

4 Bulgaria > Vitosha
5 Romania > Brasov
6 Ukraine > Sevastopol

Olympic fitness *Sochi, Russia*

For many years, Sochi (population 400,000) was the summer capital of the USSR—Stalin had his summer dacha here. But the wealthy Russians of the twentieth century prefer other destinations. Sochi has therefore diversified into a winter resort, even hosting the 2014 Winter Olympics. The Caucasus Mountains are close by: travel only 30 miles (50 km) from the coast and you can be at 9,800 feet (3,000 m). Just as in the Alps, mountain biking has become the go-to activity in the area around Sochi to turn a profit from the infrastructure originally built for winter sports. Dedicated runs have been developed on nearby Mount Akhun—2,175 feet (663 m) at its summit—from which you can see the distant shores of Turkey when conditions are clear. The densest concentration of facilities is to be found at Krasnaya Polyana, 30 minutes from Mount Akhun. Gorky Bike Park (named in homage to Arshile Gorky, the abstract expressionist painter inspired by the region, and not Maxim, the writer) provides thrills galore amid a landscape of birch trees, ferns, caves, and waterfalls. When the day's riding is done, it's time for a sauna, followed by an ice bath—a Sochi tradition—then a pot of the local Krasnodar tea.

Tackling the Great Wall

They say in China, "You're not a hero if you've not climbed the Great Wall." But not by bike! It is, of course, forbidden to cycle the Great Wall. Still, with a section of it only 50 miles (80 km) from the Forbidden City, you can cycle there from Dayangshan Forest, passing little farms, orchards, and streams until you reach Huanghuacheng Lake. It's hard to imagine that it stretches for 3,700 miles (6,000 km).

THE GIANT CHINESE BICYCLE INDUSTRY
China's hegemony over the global bicycle market

70
million
bicycles in China

1,000
companies
connected to the bicycle industry

86%
of bicycles
sold in the United States are made in China

28
million
electric bicycles sold in China each year—90% of the world market

215
million
dollars raised in 2017 by the station-less bicycle-sharing start-up Mobike

Where the city breathes *Beijing, China*

Beijing and its 21 million inhabitants have their mountains to the west and north of the megacity, beyond the sixth ring road (it's an ever-expanding series). Few of these peaks exceed 2,800 feet (1,000 m), yet they will host the 2022 Winter Olympics. Yanqing and Zhangjiakou (to the north of Beijing) have been chosen for the downhill and cross-country events, so there is no lack of mountain-biking facilities in and around the Chinese capital during the

summer. Nevertheless, you might prefer Xiangshan to the west, on the edge of the metropolitan area, between the fourth and fifth ring roads, and away from the more harmful power-station pollutants. Nine miles (15 km) to the southwest is Laoshan, which hosted the Olympic mountain-biking events in 2008. You can, however, stick to Xiangshan (literally, "Fragrant Hills"). Some of the hills form part of a superb park that is similar to a botanical

garden, where China's royal rulers would once relax. You'll ride between pines, cypresses, maple trees, and temples, such as the Biyun (Temple of Azure Clouds). Once you veer off into Badachu and Forest Park, you'll find that the paths become sportier. Mountain biking is an original way to experience Beijing.

Creative cross-country

It's not easy to find adventure on the Japanese roads—confrontations with cars aside. But a Frenchman, Emmanuel Bastian, the director of a courier firm in Strasbourg, has managed to do so since 2015. He created the Japanese Odyssey, a two-week unsupported trek across the country, from Tokyo to Osaka, visiting every corner of the archipelago and covering more than 1,240 miles (2,000 km). The only requirement is that you pass through nine obligatory segments.

SHIMANO, JAPANESE GIANT
The major dates of the leading bicycle parts manufacturer (shifters, brakes, wheels, etc.)

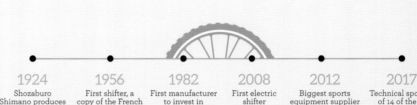

1924
Shozaburo Shimano produces his first freewheel cog in Osaka

1956
First shifter, a copy of the French Simplex model

1982
First manufacturer to invest in mountain biking, with Deore—a now legendary range

2008
First electric shifter

2012
Biggest sports equipment supplier in the world, ahead of Adidas and Nike, with a turnover of $2.7 billion

2017
Technical sponsor of 14 of the 18 teams on the pro tour

Empire of the senses *Nagano, Japan*

In Japan, all mountain-biking roads lead to Nagano, 155 miles (250 km) northwest of Tokyo. The city that hosted the 1998 Winter Olympics has exploited its mountainous topography to diversify the sporting activities on offer, with a few little extras specific to Japan: a very warm summer climate, gorgeous natural riches (waterfalls, gorges, bamboo forests, an abundance of apple plantations), and those indefinable colors that tint the landscape. Sports-wise, there are hundreds of miles of trails and paths on which to get lost in the area around Nagano and the neighboring resort of Hakuba. The mountains of Honshu (name of the principal island in the archipelago) sit imposingly on the horizon, calling you to explore their slopes: Iizuna, Fujimi (the mecca of descending), Yakikura, and the venerable Mount Tateyama (60 miles/100 km away), the only one to exceed 9,800 feet (3,000 m) and one of Japan's "Three Holy Mountains," along with Fuji and Haku. Its wild foothills are pure delight. Once the riding is done, there only remains to sample the local specialty of crickets cooked in sake, accompanied by soba noodles and soy sauce—protein and slow carbs, perfect for the following day's exertions.

Enter the Round

Since 2011, the Ronde Tahitienne event has opened up the roads along the north coast of the best known of the Windward Islands, with its lagoons and turquoise ocean, to cyclists of all types. It has three levels: leisure (9 miles/15 km), short (34 miles/55 km), and long (68 miles/110 km). Popular with riders from all over the world, the event has received the "eco cycle" label from its supervisory body, the French Cycling Federation.

A LOOP ROUND OPUNOHU VALLEY
From the pineapple road to Opunohu Valley, through breathtaking landscapes

Maharepa
Papeotai
Hauru
Vai'are
Moorea
Haapiti
Afareaitu
Vai'anae

Paopao
(Cook Bay)

Duration half a day	**Distance** 13 miles (21 km)	**Difficulty** average	**Tip** ride with a cyclist who knows the place (essential)	**Water** bring a lot with you, because of the red dust when it's dry

Between pineapples and grapefruits *Moorea, French Polynesia*

There are certain names, the simple pronunciation of which is a voyage in itself. Moorea, Tahiti's sister island in the group of Society Islands (the heart of French Polynesia), is a promise of pure escape. Moorea—"yellow lizard" in Tahitian—lies 10.5 miles (17 km) from Papeete and 143 miles (230 km) from Bora Bora and has remained authentic. This island jewel is a call to tranquility with its stunning, hibiscus-scented landscapes, lulled by the sound of the ukulele. Its rare and bountiful ecosystem, and its ancient history evoked by the ruins of numerous *marae* (sacred meeting places) make Moorea *the* timeless island. The Opunohu Valley loop takes in the majestic Opunohu and Cook Bays, allowing you to start and finish on the road that runs beside pineapple and grapefruit plantations. Start from Paopao, in the north of the island, and head south for 13 miles (21 km) along rocky trails and paths with some short climbs. The route will take you through luxuriant vegetation and fields before leading you back to the point of departure, where, red with dust, you'll plunge into one of the most beautiful lagoons in the world. Fair reward!

The great peacemaker

Road cyclists and mountain bikers have long ignored each other, occupying different worlds—that is, until a thirty-four-year-old champion raised in the Australian outback won the Tour de France in 2011. Although he first discovered the race in front of his TV at age fourteen, Cadel Evans was initially a talented mountain biker, who had twice won the World Cup. Others, such as Peter Sagan, have taken the same route. It's great the two bikes now talk to each other!

EPICALLY ALPINE
With the Australian Alpine Epic, the continent now has a sublime and very sporty mountain-biking route between Mounts Buller, Stirling, and Russell

Duration
4 to 7h

Distance
25 miles (40 km)

Difficulty
high

Height difference
+ 4,084 feet (+ 1,245 m)
- 7,175 feet (- 2,187 m)

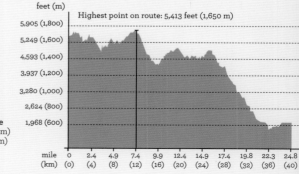

feet (m) — Highest point on route: 5,413 feet (1,650 m)

| 5,905 (1,800) |
| 5,249 (1,600) |
| 4,593 (1,400) |
| 3,937 (1,200) |
| 3,280 (1,000) |
| 2,624 (800) |
| 1,968 (600) |

mile   0   2.4   4.9   7.4   9.9   12.4 14.9 17.4 19.8 22.3 24.8
(km) (0)   (4)   (8)   (12) (16) (20) (24) (28) (32) (36) (40)

Austral giant *Mount Buller, Australia*

The Australian Alps, situated in the southeast of the country, look like modest hills compared with their European cousins. Mount Kosciuszko, Australia's highest summit, tops out at 7,310 feet (2,228 m), while nearby Mount Buller is just 5,922 feet (1,805 m). Yet it's there that the residents of Melbourne (155 miles/250 km away), Canberra, and Sydney come to ski during the southern winter in July and August.

When their summer comes at the end of the calendar year, they return to the ski lifts with their bikes. Mount Buller, in particular, enjoys a great reputation, having been transformed into a sumptuous bike park. You can practice descents ("gravity biking" for the Australians) on a multitude of trails through landscapes of savannah and forest. Aficionados of sporty cross-country and trekking will also be satisfied. Mount Buller is the focus of an

array of spirited cycle-related events into late April. The Australians in the past have been masters at making outdoor thrills a lifestyle. The Epic Trail, a route that combines endurance and technical challenge, with a succession of embankments, ramps, jumps, and crossings of streams with wooden planks, makes Mount Buller one of the most beautiful mountain-biking courses in the world.

Thrills at Ngongotaha

Mount Ngongotaha rises nearly 1,300 feet (400 m) above Lake Rotorua. It's not huge, but Skyline Gravity Park is where New Zealanders go to experience the biggest thrills in downhill biking. A gondola lift takes you to the top, from where eleven trails head downhill. Kelly McGarry, one of the craziest freeride talents, often trained here until his death in 2016 (from a cardiac arrest), at age thirty.

TE ARA AHI – HOT TRAILS
Explore Rotorua's geothermal areas

1. Rotorua and its lake
2. Other lakes
3. Whakarewarewa and its bike park
4. Waimangu Valley
5. Wai-O-Tapu
6. Waikite Valley

Duration
2 days

Distance
30 miles
(48 km)

Tip
Remember
your swimsuit

The Maori hot springs *Rotorua, New Zealand*

Why is Rotorua a leading destination in the Southern Hemisphere? This medium-sized town on New Zealand's North Island lies 125 miles (200 km) southeast of Auckland. The surrounding region has a multitude of non-mountainous cycling trails, but is also renowned for its geothermal activity. Indeed, a whiff of sulfur sometimes hangs over the town. Geysers, hot springs, and warm mud pools are never far away. All of this is found in the heart of a Maori culture, which has developed around seventeen lakes. Te Ara Ahi is the most well-known trail. Running from Rotorua to the Waikite hot springs, it passes Whakarewarewa (an ancestral Maori village that is also the setting of a superb, challenging bike park), the volcanic valley of Waimangu, and the Wai-O-Tapu hot springs. You should approach the ride as a relaxed tour rather than as a sporty endeavor. Take a moment to enjoy a refreshing dip in one of the many natural pools that you'll pass as you glide around a bend. Set aside two days for this 28-mile (45 km) ride. Shuttle buses will take you back to Rotorua. The landscape is splendidly undulating, with giant sequoias, a luxuriant forest, and a mixture of paved roads and dirt trails.

Bike Snob

Before New York City really caught the cycling bug, Eben Weiss was already riding there, observing his city and its idiosyncrasies. This gave rise to *Bike Snob*, the sharpest and funniest cycling blog in the world. It's well worth a read, either before you head to the Big Apple or simply to enjoy the barbs and witticisms of a man who loves cycling in New York so much, he now bemoans the cycling boom that makes it difficult for him to get around the city smoothly.

BROOKLYN, CYCLE CENTRAL
Six spots to really feel NYC cycling culture

1. **Brooklyn Bridge**
   view over Manhattan
2. **Bike shop**
   Redbeard Bikes, 69 Jay Street
3. **Bike coffee and shop**
   Red Lantern, 345 Myrtle Avenue
4. **Bike shop**
   Ride Brooklyn, 468 Bergen Street
5. **Bike shop** Bicycle Habitat,
   560 Vanderbilt Avenue
6. **Cycle lane**
   Around Prospect Park

New York, New York! *New York City, United States*

As a cycling city, New York is the improbable surprise of the 2010s. Gone are the days when the only crazies to pedal across Manhattan were death-defying bicycle messengers. Now, tourists are even advised to hire a bike to see New York, instead of taking the subway or a cab. Janette Sadik-Khan, the former commissioner of the New York City Department of Transportation under Michael Bloomberg (mayor from 2002 to 2013)

is responsible for putting in place a solid cycling culture across the five boroughs, including 400 miles of bike lanes and the Citi Bike bicycle sharing program, which was introduced in 2013 and now counts 12,000 bikes and more than 700 stations. The Bike Access to Office Buildings Law allows employees in commercial office buildings to bring their bikes into their offices by freight elevator. Where once the only cycling spot was Central Park, now it's the entire city.

Brooklyn, with its dense network of cycle lanes and go-to bike shops, is perhaps the real heart of contemporary cycle culture in the Big Apple.

Divvy, child of Paris

It was summer 2007. Chicago had just launched an Olympic bid, and Mayor Richard M. Daley was traveling the world seeking support. While in Paris, he was invited by the Paris mayor Bertrand Delanoë to test the recently introduced Vélib' bike share program. Daley was won over and took the idea back with him. His Divvy bike-share program in Chicago was key to the city being named America's Top City for Cycling by *Bicycling* magazine in 2016.

THE TIKI TOUR
One of the most fun cycle tours in Chicago, getting a taste of Hawaiian culture

Start
at the speakeasy
Three Dots and a Dash

Pit stop
at the Lost Lake to sample
Bunny's Banana Daiquiri

Finish
at the Hala Kahiki Lounge for a
Hala Kahiki served in a whole
frozen pineapple

0 km ●----------------------●----------------------● 21 km

A long cycling heritage *Chicago, United States*

In the Windy City, cyclists pedal happily between the skyscrapers of the Loop—the central business district—as well as on the cycle paths beside Lake Michigan, with the city skyline behind them, or on Milwaukee Avenue—dubbed "Hipster Highway." Everywhere, in fact, and with few restrictions. Cycling in Chicago has a long history. As far back as 1900, before the appearance of the motor car, the capital of Illinois was already a major cycling center with more than fifty cycle clubs that together had more than ten thousand members. It is said that even the city's thirtieth mayor, Carter Harrison Jr., was a member of one of these clubs. In modern times, two other mayors have done much to maintain and progress this heritage. Richard J. Daley drove the construction of the first cycle paths in the 1970s, while his eldest son, Richard M. Daley, has brought bicycling Chicago into the twenty-first century.

By 2020, there will be 620 miles of cycle paths. At the McDonald's Cycle Center, a unique place in the northeast corner of Millennium Park, you can lock up your bike, learn to repair it, or take a shower before heading to work. Farther south is Chicago's chicest bike café, aptly named Heritage Bicycles.

The memory of a pioneer

Running parallel to the main shopping street, Rue Sainte-Catherine, is Boulevard de Maisonneuve, which traverses downtown Montreal. Its cycle lane is named "Claire Morissette" in homage to the cycling advocate who in the 1980s urged city hall to include cycling and cyclists in their planning. Claire Morissette departed too soon, taken by breast cancer at 57, but cyclists of Montreal will never forget her.

MONTREAL TO LACHINE
One of the loveliest urban rides in the world

Route
From the Old Port of Montreal to Parc René-Lévesque in Lachine

Direction
West

See
Atwater Market and Parc Saint-Louis

Distance
14 miles (22 km)

Four seasons challenge *Montreal, Canada*

Vélo d'hiver ("winter cycling") is the pretty Québécois expression applied to the activity of thousands of cyclists who don't abandon their favorite mode of transport just because Montreal lies under the snow, and the temperature is below freezing. You gear up and dress right. Sometimes you even flout restrictions, such as taking the cycle path on the venerable Jacques-Cartier Bridge, which is closed when icy. Half of the cycle paths in Montreal (267 miles/ 430 km) are classed as "four season." Such is Montrealers's appetite for cycling that from November to April, snow-clearers make sure these cycle paths are safe to ride. There are a million cyclists aged 3 to 75 in Montreal (half the population) and a million and a half bicycles. Around 60% of the under-35s use their bike at least four hours a week, and more than four million weekly journeys by bike were tallied up in 2016. Montrealers love to celebrate cycling, particularly when joy fills the city as the first buds announce the return of spring. The capital of Québec certainly deserves its title of North America's cycling capital.

Cyclists bare all

Nowhere but Portland has such a fun and exuberant festival as Pedalpalooza, which takes place over the three weeks preceding July 4. The Naked Ride is the most famous event of the festival, with 10,000 participants in 2016, and the concept has been extended to other events across the world. There is a serious subliminal message: a cyclist might as well be naked, in light of the danger posed by a motor car.

BIKE AND HIKE
When touring Portland by bike, be sure to take a detour via Rocky Butte

Joseph Wood Hill Park
encompasses this volcanic cone, with several networks of trails to ride

Most of the stones used for the stairs and walls dotted around Rocky Butte come from the cone itself

Watch the sun set over Mount Hood from the stone wall

612 feet (187 m)
Height of Rocky Butte

Green and right-on *Portland, United States*

Flowers and bicycles. It's a striking image when you arrive in Portland, Oregon. This holds true even outside of the two weeks in April when the cherry blossoms in the Portland Japanese Garden put on their impressive show. Rhododendrons, roses, and azaleas flower in such profusion that you'd never think that you were in a city of 600,000 inhabitants. Situated an hour's drive from the ocean, Portland is a city that breathes. It is considered to be

America's greenest city, as well as having the highest number of vegetarian restaurants. The climate is mild; the city is surrounded by forests and waterways and is traversed by the Willamette River, with the Columbia River not far away. A natural craving for the outdoors saw Nike grow huge in the 1970s, from their Beaverton base a few miles west of downtown Portland. In memory of that heritage, the company has spent ten million dollars since 2012 developing

BikeTown, Portland's orange bike-share program. On the superb Tilikum Crossing, a cable-stayed bridge over the Willamette River, you will find electric buses, pedestrians, and cyclists, but no cars, which are forbidden from using it. Life is good in Portland.

"Battling" mayors

Enrique Peñalosa, leader of the Green Party and mayor of Bogotá from 1998 to 2001 and again since 2015, wears his humanist values on his sleeve. "For a city to prosper," he said, "its inhabitants must feel at ease there. Bicycle use contributes to that." He believes so strongly in this that he indulges in regular friendly "battles" on social media with Federico Gutiérrez, mayor of rival city Medellín.

BOGOTÁ, A CYCLING REVOLUTION
The infrastructure created for sustainable transport (bicycles) has changed the lives of Bogotans

70%
of the city's population
don't own a motor vehicle, mainly because they can't afford one

230
miles
(374 km) of cycle paths, which extend to the neighborhoods farthest from the center

2
million
daily journeys by bicycle in Bogotá is the aim for 2025

23%
of the city's population
say they use a bicycle in Bogotá for its rapidity

Sunday night fever *Bogotá, Colombia*

It's a unique phenomenon: La Ciclovia gifts Bogotans more than 60 miles (100 km) of its most beautiful roads and wide avenues, car-free, every Sunday morning. Up to a million citizens take advantage of this to explore the city— some on foot, others on roller skates, but the vast majority by bike. La Ciclovia was created in the 1970s by Ortiz Marino, a highly civic-minded activist, who was aghast at the amount of space cars were taking up in his city.

He had the pioneering idea of a gathering of cyclists as a counterpoint. It was an immediate success. The concept led to a marvelous degree of social mixing and taste for cycling in Bogotá, which has resulted in many huge climbing talents reaching the Tour de France. Curiously, though, in 2016, only 4% of the city's inhabitants used a bicycle to get to work, perhaps because of Bogotá's highly effective bus rapid transit system, TransMilenio,

and despite 230 miles (374 km) of cycle paths. Nevertheless, any visitor should take advantage of the cycle infrastructure. From the historic neighborhood of La Candelaria, with its Gold Museum and cobblestone streets, 6 miles (10 km) of cycle paths run along prestigious Carrera Septima (Seventh Street) to Catacion Publica, where you can sample the finest coffee in Bogotá.

La playera endures

In the streets of Buenos Aires, you can still see many *playeras* (beach cruisers). Invented in the United States in the 1930s, these single-speed bikes with oversized handlebars, balloon tires, and a relaxed upright seat position found a new lease of life in Argentina. A *playera* is slow, handles like a shopping cart, and has a questionable appearance. If you're after a secondhand one, take a look at the very popular Facebook page Intercambio de Bicicletas.

BUENOS AIRES, PLEASURE ON TWO WHEELS
The Argentinian capital is particularly well-suited to exploration by bike

6
miles
(10 km) from Belgrano to La
Boca, the best of Buenos Aires

14th
in the 2016 world ranking
of bike-friendly cities

4th
in the ranking
of major cities whose bike use
increased the most in 2016

12,000
free-to-use bikes
Early 2017

Playera, or beach cruiser

180,000
daily bike journeys

Tango colors *Buenos Aires, Argentina*

On picturesque, colorful Caminito Street in the La Boca neighborhood, they say that tango never stops. The same might be said for cycling across the Argentinian capital. There has been a real bicycle craze in Buenos Aires since 2009, due largely to the clever decision on the part of the authorities to make their EcoBici bike-share program entirely free to use—something that has not been done anywhere else. There are 120 miles (200 km) of bike lanes in

Buenos Aires. Most are along relatively quiet roads, but you must take great care crossing the avenues, where the motor car reigns supreme. Still, you can enjoy a fine day's cycling across the city, from the chic northern neighborhoods to those in the south—which mix tradition and modernity. The trick is not to get too far from the ocean. You'll pass the bustle of Belgrano, the tranquility of Palermo Woods park, the cultural ferment of Recoleta, the

bohemian vibes of San Telmo, and the hip Puerto Madero Waterfront. Or else ride across the pedestrian Woman's Bridge (bicycles allowed), an ode to the new Argentinian society.

The jagged bike path

Without a doubt, it was the most beautiful cycle path in the world, with an unbeatable view. It was constructed at the foot of a cliff, only a few feet above the Atlantic, south of Leblon Beach, and formed the prolongation of a marvelous promenade. It may have been built too hurriedly; in April 2016, the stormy ocean swept away the construction, and two cyclists lost their lives. Since then, Brazil has taken cycle safety more seriously.

VIA COPACABANA AND IPANEMA
Fourteen unforgettable miles (23 km), from Sugarloaf Mountain to Pedra da Gavea, via the beaches.

● Leme > Copacabana, **1.8 miles** (2.8 km)

● Copacabana > Ipanema, **2 miles** (3.1 km)

● Ipanema > Leblon, **2 miles** (3.1 km)

● Leblon > Vidigal, **1.5 miles** (2.5 km)

● Vidigal > Pedra da Gavea, **7.5 miles** (12.2 km)

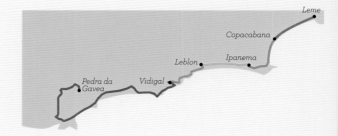

Samba on two wheels *Rio de Janeiro, Brazil*

Silence, space, nature, landscape: words that describe the experience of cycling in Rio, whether riding beside the mosaics and shacks of the famous Copacabana promenade or elsewhere. Cycling should have been an obvious activity here, before the 2010s and the environmental policies accompanying the Football World Cup and the Olympic Games—long before the Brazilian political class descended into the chaos of corruption. Economic recession hit, and cycling benefited, once the costs of having a car, along with parking and an avalanche of traffic tickets, became a ridiculous luxury for the average Carioca. Who remembers their first rides along the brand-new cycle paths beside their favorite beaches, from Leme to Leblon, in the 1990s? There are now 190 miles (300 km) of them. The distances are so long between the neighborhoods and the stretches of luxuriant vegetation— anchored tight in the city like nowhere else—that the use of electrically assisted bikes has become a reality. Rio loves cycling—not just because of the city's climate. On Sundays, the sportier types will ride as far as the heights of Tijuca Forest, whereas the less adventurous will pedal from the Rio de Janeiro Botanical Garden around the heart-shaped Rodrigo de Freitas Lagoon.

The mysterious Bike Man

Are you looking for a secondhand bike in Dublin? Forget the usual channels and get in touch with Paul, otherwise known as "Dublin Bike Man." He'll arrange to meet you at pretty Temple Bar—Essex Street, to be precise. You'll need to have picked a bike from his very basic website in advance and pay cash. Dublin Bike Man is a controversial figure. Where do his bikes come from? One thing is for sure: his unique approach to business seems to have been unaffected by the financial crisis.

CLIMB TO THREE ROCK
Bike up the "mountain" south of Dublin (with its three huge rocks), which sits 1,457 feet (444 m) above the Irish Sea. From there, you'll get a marvelous view over the city.

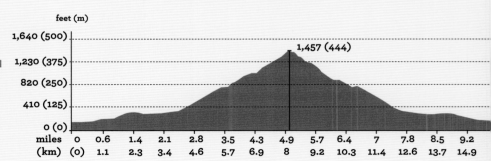

feet (m)							1,457 (444)					
1,640 (500)												
1,230 (375)												
820 (250)												
410 (125)												
0 (0)												
miles	0	0.6	1.4	2.1	2.8	3.5	4.3	4.9	5.7	6.4	7	7.8	8.5	9.2
(km)	(0)	1.1	2.3	3.4	4.6	5.7	6.9	8	9.2	10.3	11.4	12.6	13.7	14.9

Celtic fervor *Dublin, Ireland*

The Irish are never ones to lag behind the British. The bicycle's conquest of London in the years before the 2012 Olympics inspired Dublin. Between a plate of fish and chips, "a small one" (whiskey, of course), and a ballad, Dubliners like to pedal. The city has 75 miles (120 km) of segregated bike lanes and 30 miles (50 km) of shared bus lanes to make riding around the city pleasant and safe. As long as you stay in town, you will not find a hill to climb.

The Dublinbikes bike-share program had 70,000 subscribers in 2016, but the nonprofit service aroused some controversy when it received sponsorship from Coca-Cola Zero, the logo of which still adorned the bikes in 2017. Was it an offense to the land of Guinness? Still, the program is a practical way of visiting the architectural riches and green spaces of Dublin, a "little town" of 500,000 inhabitants, where one immediately feels at ease.

From Trinity College to the castle south of the Liffey River, and from the cycle path by the Grand Canal to the magnificent Phoenix Park in the north, the most attractive routes are now open to bicycles. Along the way, you'll experience the unique energy of Ireland's proud capital.

A Sunday in Germany

It's the favorite weekend destination for residents of Strasbourg: cycling over the very contemporary Mimram bridge (no cars) to Kehl, the town's German neighbor. Three miles (5 km) from the cathedral, the bridge crosses the Rhine—on both sides of which lies the Jardin des Deux-Rives, a symbol of Franco-German harmony. Five more minutes and you're in Kehl where the cakes at Café Backhaus Dreher are to die for!

A RIDE AROUND THE FORTS

A 50-mile (85 km) tour of the ring of forts around Strasbourg, starting from the Parc de l'Orangerie tram station

5
of the 19 original forts can be visited

1 mile
(1.6 km)
Shortest section

6.5 miles
(10.4 km)
Longest section

1,049 feet
(320 m)
altitude gain

Beautiful Petite France *Strasbourg, France*

You should arrive in Strasbourg by train. Once you've walked out from under the vast glass canopy of the central station, stop to contemplate the vision of hundreds of bicycles padlocked to bike stands or locked together. You'd think you were in Amsterdam! Strasbourg is a cycling town, no doubt about it. It is by far the most advanced in France, and it is the fourth most bicycle-friendly city in Europe, according to the 2017 ranking drawn up by the Danish organization Copenhagenize. There is something very peaceful about Strasbourg, particularly its island center and surrounding streets—from the cathedral to the picturesque Petite France. Cycling conquered the city in the 1990s, accompanying the renovation of the streetcar system. Every canal and every main street has been given its own separate bike lane—370 miles (600 km) in 2017. Employers cover half of the annual subscription for the Vélhop bike-share program, which can also be prescribed by a doctor. Being this close to Germany, you're not far from a network of greenways. There are a number of nonprofits teaching cycling as a tool of "emancipation," particularly for women from immigrant backgrounds. Strasbourg is looking far ahead down the cycle path.

Look, no hands!

It's the essential rallying point for London cyclists, and much more besides: Look Mum No Hands! has taken the "bike cafe" concept to the extreme. Here, you can buy a bike, get your ride repaired, eat, drink, work, chat, and watch major cycling events on a big screen. If you're a pedalhead visiting the Big Smoke, you simply have to drop in to Look mum no hands! The original establishment on Old Street now has a little brother close to Tower Bridge called Lmnh Kitchen.

SECRETS OF THE THAMES
An astonishing 16-mile (27 km) ride along the water

LONDON

1 Tate Modern (museum)
2 Palestra House
3 The Old Vic (theater)
4 Tower Bridge
5 Ornamental Canal
6 Prospect of Whitby (pub)
7 Canary Wharf

8 Island Gardens
9 Greenland Dock
10 Stave Hill
11 Manor House (ruins)
12 Borough Market and Southwark Cathedral

Mini Holland, max pleasure *London, United Kingdom*

It would once have been an incongruous sight to see a cyclist rolling down Piccadilly or through the city between black cabs and red buses. Things changed in the early twenty-first century, when cycling became an everyday activity in London, thanks largely to the policies put in place by the last three mayors to combat the city's pollution, gridlock, and dangerous roads. The Labour mayor Ken Livingstone got things moving by taking advantage of the highly publicized events to be held in London over the following years: the start of the 2007 Tour de France and the 2012 Olympics. When the Conservative mayor Boris Johnson came to power, he injected some blue into his environmental policy through his bike-share program and the color of the road paint used for the first "cycle superhighways," which were wide, dedicated lanes. When London swung back to Labour in 2016 with Sadiq Khan, this momentum continued. Between now and 2020, 770 million pounds will be invested in cycling infrastructure, including several Mini Hollands—neighborhoods with a dense network of cycle lanes and related highway improvements. No other city in the world has spent as much money on cycling. The pioneering Cycle Superhighway 3 starts out in the east of the city at Barking, before swooping in via Tower Bridge and Westminster to end west of Hyde Park. These are good times to be a cyclist in London.

Windmills of Zaanse Schans

It's far too tempting to cycle everywhere in the Netherlands. Ride north out of Amsterdam for 9 miles (15 km) along cycle paths beside canals and the Zaan River. After barely an hour of pleasant pedaling, you'll reach Zaanse Schans, one of the most picturesque traditional Dutch "windmill villages" that you'll ever see, thanks to a number of well-preserved historic windmills and houses having been relocated here in the 1960s. It's a free outdoor museum. April to October is the best time to visit, when all the windmills are open to the public.

AMSTERDAM, CITY OF EVERY EXCESS
Lots of bicycles, thefts, and insufficient bike parking

600,000
bikes (for 750,000 inhabitants)

40,000
more parking spots for bikes between now and 2030

250 miles
(400 km)
of bike lanes and paths

40,000
bike thefts reported each year

Inimitable charm *Amsterdam, the Netherlands*

A canal and several elegant "Dutch" bikes parked before a backdrop of seventeenth-century facades. If you were looking for a single image to encapsulate the ideal of cycling in an urban environment, you would find it here. Amsterdam converted itself to two wheels long before anywhere else. Cycling has now become deeply associated with the inimitable charm of this unique city. Nothing is ever far away in Amsterdam, where there are nearly

as many bicycles as there are inhabitants. Here, a red road surface tells the user that they're in a 20 mph (30 km/h) zone, which is reassuring. At each traffic light, there's a mirror to enable car drivers to see cyclists in their blind spots. Children learn how to ride a bike and about cycling etiquette at day care. "Black spots" are identified and modified if six accidents are recorded in less than three years. Amsterdam has given its soul to cycling, and it's by bike

that you should explore the city. Start in Jordaan, the bohemian bourgeois neighborhood, and pedal to Dam Square, then head to Museumplein to see Rembrandt, Vermeer, Van Gogh, and other Dutch masters, or to Vondelpark to stretch out on the grass before lingering in a coffee shop. Amsterdam is yours—by bike, of course! You've only just begun.

129

At the foot of the mountains

Jammed between the Adriatic, Italy, Austria, Hungary, and Croatia, with a surface area half that of Switzerland, Slovenia is a country of short distances. No sooner are you out of Ljubljana than you're in the foothills of the Dolomites. A short and pleasant ride will take you to the highly innovative Podutik Bike Park, which opened in 2015. Go there with a mountain bike and knock yourself out. It will only cost you 15 euros.

MTB ON THE HILL
A ride toward Mali Rožnik and its woods, adjacent to Tivoli Park

Duration
2h

Distance
8 miles
(13 km)

Difficulty
easy to
average

Altitude gain
1,200 feet
(365 m)

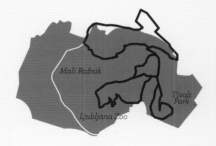

Promise of the Balkans *Ljubljana, Slovenia*

At night, bicycles roll smoothly through the quiet streets of Ljubljana, where cars have been banned from the historic center with its baroque and art nouveau architecture. There are thousands of bicycles here, even though Slovenia's capital—the Switzerland of the Balkans—has fewer than 300,000 inhabitants. You should remember that in the former Yugoslavia, the bicycle was the mode of transport for workers and farmers, so cycle culture is firmly rooted here. You should also remember that, in the 1990s, a local architect, Edvard Ravnikar, concerned about the increase in motor traffic, went to Copenhagen to see how they had integrated the bicycle into the city. He applied the lessons learned upon his return, and today, Ljubljana is a real cycling city—and not just around Dragon Bridge and the cathedral— inspiring the neighboring cities of Celje and Maribor. There are 50 miles (80 km) of cycle paths and just as many bike lanes. On Avenue Dunajska, there's a meter indicating that 5,000 bicycles descend from the north of the city to the center every day of the week. Pretty Tivoli Park to the east now has a cycle path. In 2016, Ljubljana received the European Green Capital Award. Bicycles continue to roll smoothly here.

A godsend for the economy

Seville has seen an explosion of bicycle tourism. There's something for everyone. You only have to ride out of town toward Cádiz, Malaga, or Cordoba to find sportier terrain—all year round too, for the mercury never drops below 50°F (10°C). Better still, since 2010, the number of specialist stores has increased from ten to fifty. Some, such as Santa Cleta, provide free training to job seekers wanting to become bike mechanics.

THE JEWEL THAT IS PLAZA DE ESPAÑA

Movies
A scene from *Star Wars: Episode II: Attack of the Clones* was filmed here

.5 million sq. ft.
(50,000 m²)
surface area (palace and moat combined)

1914–1928
Period of its construction

West
Direction the square faces, toward the Guadalquivir River, symbol of the route to the Americas

Beautiful Andalusia *Seville, Spain*

The flamenco dress is still a hit in this town, but the twenty-first century sevillana only takes it out of the wardrobe for a *feria*. The rest of the time, she gets around by bicycle, wearing a more suitable, yet no less elegant, outfit. If there was one setting we might have dreamed about pedaling our beloved bike, Seville might be at the top of the list. Could there be a more sumptuous ride than from the Triana Bridge to Plaza de España and then the cathedral? The traffic circulation plans conceived for the west bank of the Guadalquivir, on the occasion of Seville Expo '92, opened the way. José García Cebrián and Manuel Calvo, the men responsible for sustainable mobility at city hall, were both die-hard cyclists. Nowadays, Seville, the cycling capital of Southern Europe, has a bike-share program of 3,000 bicycles, while nearly 100,000 bicycles circulate every day on 75 miles (120 km) of special lanes, colored green. Most of these are accessible from the sidewalks and are protected by a low fence. Here, in the land of bullfighting, some cyclists still fear being "gored" by a car at certain junctions.

The future is coming

"We all cycle" is the slogan of Utrecht's cycling initiative. In 2015, 180 of the city's residents were recruited to plan the infrastructure of tomorrow. The aim was to overtake Amsterdam and Copenhagen to become the most bike-friendly city on the planet! The first step has been to develop a technology to allow everyone to use their smartphone to find the nearest bike park with free spaces.

Day 1: Utrecht > Weesp, **25 miles** (40 km)
Day 2: Weesp > Nieuwkoop, **18 miles** (30 km)
Day 3: Nieuwkoop > Utrecht, **25 miles** (40 km)

Duration
less than 3h
per day

Distance
68 miles
(110 km)

Difficulty
easy

Gear
all types of bikes

The new model *Utrecht, the Netherlands*

Whoever climbs to the top of the famous Dom Tower, which at 369.5 feet (112.5 m) is the tallest church tower in the Netherlands, might experience a certain dizziness. Below, there stretches a multitude of lines and colored strips indicating cycle lanes and paths, along with thousands of bicycles whizzing through the streets. The Netherlands's fourth-largest city is full of ancestral charm with its canals, medieval streets, café terraces that have almost a

Mediterranean feel, and its student life, which is fueled by one of the most reputed universities in Europe. Above all, Utrecht, with its 400,000 inhabitants, is a cycling city. Around 40% of the tens of thousands of passengers who each morning flock to the central station— the country's second busiest—come by bike. Utrecht will soon boast the largest bike park in the world, once all the circulation routes have been laid and the multiple bridges and numerous

tunnels have been constructed. By 2020, the underground level of the Jaarbeurs convention center will have 30,000 parking spots for bikes, arranged on three levels of the most up-to-date sliding racks. Utrecht clearly intends to maintain its status as *the* European city to explore by bike.

A short ride to Venice

Bicycles are forbidden in Venice because the streets
are too narrow and there are too many people. You
can, however, reach it from the seaside town of
Chioggia at the southern end of the Venetian Lagoon,
25 miles (40 km) southwest of Padua. Cycle along
Pellestrina, an island so narrow that you'll sometimes
have to ride single file, then take a ferry to the Lido
di Venezia, before cycling all the way up this narrow
sandbar. Leave your bike and catch a vaporetto that
will deposit you at the Piazza San Marco.

THE VENETIAN LAGOON
Reach Venice via Chioggia: a pleasant ride beside the Lagoon

Duration
2h

Difficulty
easy

118
little islands
make up Venice

Venice and its
lagoon are a
UNESCO World
Heritage Site

Bici and dolce vita *Padua, Italy*

The Veneto region is the cradle of the prestigious Italian bicycle industry. Still, you don't expect to discover the most cyclable town in the country at its epicenter, halfway between the flamboyant cities of Verona and Venice. In 2016, 17% of daily journeys in Padua were made by bike—much more than in Milan, Rome, or Turin. The fact that Padua is a university city with more than 50,000 students (one-fifth of the population) has certainly got something to do with it. Distances are short, and one of the oldest universities in the world—founded in the thirteenth century—is still housed in the Palazzo Bo, right in the center. Since 2010, more than 60 miles (100 km) of bike paths have been laid as part of the ambitious Bici Masterplan. Padua is also a place where people like to cycle for pleasure—including outside the city, along the various waterways—just as much as for practical purposes, if not more so. You will never tire of this thoroughly Italian city and its maze of narrow streets winding between the towers of medieval palaces, church domes, and arcades of buildings laden with history. Then sip a Spritz on the Prato della Valle, a vast and beautiful square where a popular bicycle festival is held each April.

Social cycling

Nothing embodies the Copenhagen of tomorrow like the renovation of the Nordhavn harbor area. For a start, the two-way bike lanes are 20 feet (6 m) wide. Indeed, most of the cycling infrastructure in the Danish capital allows people to ride three abreast, meaning that a cyclist can safely overtake two others locked deep in conversation, which they call a "social cycling."

IN DENMARK, THE BICYCLE RULES
Go for it!

7,450 miles
(12,000 km)
of cycle paths

30 miles
(50 km)
maximum distance
from the sea

557 feet
(170 m)
highest point!

West
Direction from which
comes the prevailing wind
in Denmark: plan your
itinerary accordingly

Capital of the fortunates *Copenhagen, Denmark*

Copenhagen has embraced cycling with such dedication and joy that you can see the results from the sky. If you look through the airplane window as you land, you can sometimes make out lines of electric blue—the bike-only zones at intersections—and others of orange or green—the bike lanes that crisscross the city. As you walk out of the airport, you'll find that all taxis are obliged to carry your bike for a fee of 50 cents. In Copenhagen, traffic lights are synchronized according to the speed of cyclists. In fact, 150 million euros have been spent on cycling infrastructure since 2005. Several superb bridges have been constructed for cyclists alone, such as the Cykelslangen ("Cycle Snake"), or the Inner Harbour bridge, nicknamed the "Kissing Bridge," which connects the Nyhavn neighborhood with its colorful facades to the residential Christianshavn neighborhood. As a tourist, a bicycle is the best way to see the Little Mermaid, the Tivoli Gardens, and the Church of Our Savior with its famous external spiral staircase that winds around the spire. Copenhagen lives by the bicycle. Four out of five inhabitants of the first major world city to have more bikes than cars are of the opinion that cycling every day has a positive effect on the atmosphere of the city. And this is in Denmark, which is already a great place to live.

Berliners for bike lanes

In 2016, a referendum was organized by a green collective to force the municipality to implement an even more ambitious cycling plan: 280 miles (450km) of new bike lanes (a quarter of which are for "fast" users), with every avenue given a bike lane at least 6 feet (2 m) wide, traffic lights synchronized to bike speeds, and so on. A chance to catch up with Copenhagen? Why not?

VAST CITIES!
Berlin has a surface area eight times that of Paris, but other European capitals are larger still

Paris
40 mi²
(105 km²)

Berlin
344 mi²
(891 km²)

Rome
496 mi²
(1,285 km²)

London
610 mi²
(1,579 km²)

Vibrant metropolis *Berlin, Germany*

You feel something unique when you cross Berlin. From the remnants of the Wall to the Reichstag, from the Brandenburg Gate to the vestiges of the old East Germany, you can really sense the extent to which this city has witnessed so much of modern European history. Then there is the buzz of its cultural and artistic scene, as you ride away from the elegant Potsdamer Platz. And finally, all that space: Berlin is eight times larger than Paris and is built around water and parks. So you might as well explore it by bike, something that's very easy to do. Its avenues are wide and safe. Some of them date from the Imperial period: others from the Communist era. Berlin is a flat city, and many of its old cobbled streets have been paved over just for cyclists. Although there are hardly any hills, you can end up cycling a long way, so think about renting an electric bicycle from the renowned Fat Tire for only 25 euros, or else take your bike on the metro or train for only 1.50 euros. All the green spaces are open to cyclists: try the magnificent Tiergarten, Berlin's large central park. Drivers here are attentive to cyclists because most of them are cyclists too, even if only occasionally. Almost every building has its own lockable bike store. In short, Berlin is a cyclist's paradise.

Between zebras and rhinoceroses

Multiple winner of the Tour de France Chris Froome grew up in Johannesburg. Each year, he returns here and rides his favorite route through the Suikerbosrand Nature Reserve, which is 45 miles (70 km) of rolling terrain with zebras, rhinoceroses, and baboons. The most difficult aspect is cycling there from "Joburg." Froome has a trick: he leaves at six in the morning before the first traffic jam.

CYCLING IN JOHANNESBURG
A slow conquest

1
out
of every 500 journeys in
the city is by bike

25%
growth
in the population
expected by 2030

200
cyclists
from the Diepsloot
neighborhood ride to work as
a group so they're more easily
noticed by drivers

5,000
bicycles collected
each year for the
children of Soweto by the
Qhubeka foundation

27,000
participants
in the 2013 Momentum
94.7 cycle challenge,
a record

Ride to Soweto *Johannesburg, South Africa*

Cycling in "Joburg" remains a project, a dream. The concept is making progress, although not so fast that the emblematic Nelson Mandela Bridge — the contemporary lines of which link the business districts of Braamfontein and Newtown — is closed to anyone but cyclists. Never mind. The 2010 FIFA World Cup held in South Africa did help a little. In the course of fact-finding trips around the world, its organizers realized that cycling could transform their city.

Joburg experiences considerable traffic congestion; the car is king, despite only a tiny proportion of its ten million inhabitants being able to afford one. Cycling gets taught at school, even though it's not something that the poorest families care about. Bike lanes have been marked out; the first were on Mooki Street in Soweto. Homage is paid to Nelson Mandela during an annual Freedom Race from the high-rises of Sandton to Soweto. Commuter cyclists liaise on WhatsApp to ride in groups to gain a little respect from the less-than-scrupulous drivers of minibus taxis. Johannesburg is aiming for the honorary title of First Bike Friendly Metropolis on the African continent.

Battle of the cycle rickshaws

Pedicabs enchant tourists as they roll through the chic neighborhoods of New York and Paris. Meanwhile, its glorious ancestor, the cycle rickshaw, has been seeing some tough times in Jakarta and Yogyakarta. The authorities there have been clamping down on the manufacture and sale of this highly popular means of transport, owing to its harmful impact on traffic. The Indonesian rickshaw pedalers and their customers carry on regardless.

YOGYAKARTA REGION
Ride out to explore the two most important Buddhist sites in Indonesia:
Borobudur and Prambanan

Borobudur complex
Dates from the eighth and ninth centuries
72 stupas house as many statues of the Buddha

Prambanan complex
Dates from the tenth century
Six temples: three dedicated to Shiva, Vishnu, and Brahma, and three dedicated to the animals that served as their mounts (Nandi, Garuda, and Hamsa)

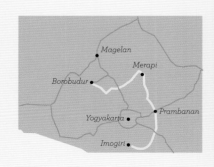

Beside the paddy fields *Yogyakarta, Indonesia*

Yes, it's a town—one where bicycles are welcomed. It's a place where you simply won't resist the temptation to ride out as soon as you arrive. Yogyakarta is the second-largest conurbation in Indonesia, situated in the middle of the island of Java, 310 miles (500 km) from Jakarta. With its 700,000 inhabitants, it's human in scale, and its character does the rest. This is the spiritual heart of the country. Bicycles are accepted by moped riders—kings of the asphalt and the main road users—which is important to bear in mind. Relics of the past and the very pleasant surroundings are but a glimpse of what you'll find once you begin to explore Yogyakarta. The temples are most astounding, such as Borobudur, fifteen minutes to the northwest, and Prambanan to the east. To the north, the horizon is magnified by the imposing silhouette of Mount Merapi, a smoking volcano. Above all, it's the pleasure of riding between rice paddies and palm groves with luxuriant nature all around. Rent a bike in Yogyakarta and go and lose yourself in the outskirts. You'll always find a bowl of *gudeg*—a delicious local recipe of young jackfruit, stewed with palm sugar and coconut milk—and a farmer to show you the way home.

Exercise before breakfast

The trend of MAMIL (middle-aged men in lycra) indulging in sports cycling exists in Delhi too. You can join the Noida Cycling Club or Delhi Cyclists for a ride. Groups head out from the Hotel Chanakya first thing on Saturdays and Sundays, taking advantage of the early morning coolness. Rides often end with a shared breakfast of *idlis* (steamed cakes made of rice and lentils), curried mutton, and chai (spiced black tea with milk).

EXPLORE NEW DELHI BY BIKE
The journalist Atish Patel gives a few tips for making the most of a bike ride in the Indian capital.

5:30 a.m.
The ideal time to ride in summer (quiet roads and a cooler temperature)

Watch it!
Out on the road, it's the size of the vehicle (and the horns) that counts

Friends
Cycle in a group for a safer ride

Break
Lots of green spaces for cyclists to relax

Early in Delhi *New Delhi, India*

In India, pedaling usually means a cycle rickshaw—that multicolored tricycle used to transport both people and goods. They fill the street in front of India Gate, a monument to the Indian dead of World War I that serves as a local reference point. Add the thick scooter traffic and randomly wandering cows (sacred animals here), and it's difficult to see a way to cycle through it all. Yet, New Delhi, which was laid out a century ago when the British moved the administrative capital here from Kolkata, has inherited one advantage: very wide avenues. The Rajpath, or "King's Way," which links India Gate to the former British viceroy's palace (now the current residence of India's president), is the first stretch to explore by bike. It is imperative to set off early in the day to avoid the traffic and heat. "Early" means 5:30 a.m. in India. It's the magic hour when Delhi awakes. There is much to choose from in Delhi. Why not take the gravel path through Sanjay Van Forest, or another to Mangar Lake? Or explore the fascinating urban treasures of the heart of Delhi, such as the Lutyens' Delhi quarter—named after the architect of New Delhi—or the contemporary Lotus Temple, the tree-lined avenues of Pusa Hill Forest, the Garden of Five Senses, or the banks of the Yamuna River. It's all a few pedal turns away, but do leave to explore them early.

147

Bike-share 2.0

A symbol of the Cultural Revolution, the bicycle had been falling out of favor in China since the capitalist era and the rise of the motor car. It has seen a rebirth, thanks to new technology that has won over a younger user base. The firms Mobike, which took the first step in Shanghai, and Ofo have revolutionized bike-sharing. You no longer have to take a bicycle from one station and then leave it at another. You can simply lock it and leave it wherever you like by using a smartphone app. The downside, however, is that it has led to piles of abandoned bikes across Chinese cities.

THE "FREE BIKE" EXPLOSION
The number of free bike programs by continent, as of late 2016

Europe 524

Asia 502

North America 121

Central America 34

Oceania 6

Africa 1

Lake of marvels *Hangzhou, China*

China's polluted and smog-smothered cities are no longer thronged with bicycles as they were in the past. There are some rare exceptions, such as Hangzhou, 95 miles (150 km) south of Shanghai, which is nicknamed "the Green City." It does, of course, boast the usual urban sprawl: a central business district of high-rises, a futuristic train station that is the size of an airport, and even a neighborhood of Paris-style buildings, complete with a replica of the Eiffel Tower. But it still retains something of the character of Marco Polo when he arrived here in the late thirteenth century. "The finest and most splendid city in the world" was what Polo wrote about Hangzhou, then the capital of the Song dynasty. In Hangzhou, you can rent one of 70,000 bicycles parked at nearly 3,000 stations; in 2016, it was the largest such bike-share program in the world. Pedal west, away from the bay, toward the mountain slopes where they plant longjing tea and enjoy a lovely ride around West Lake amid luxuriant vegetation, over half-moon bridges, and past sublime pagodas. It's a moment of respite from the bustle of urban China. Hangzhou may be ranked thirteenth in the country for population size, but it is without a doubt the first when it comes to the pleasure of pedaling.

Krylatskoye, in memory of the Olympics

Fancy a sporty ride? Cycle to the nearby hills of Krylatskoye (west of central Moscow), where a protected 8-mile (13 km) loop is a souvenir of the 1980 Olympics—the course of the road race won by Sergei Sukhoruchenkov, the greatest Soviet cyclist of all time. He was an unknown competitor before the Olympics because cyclists from the Eastern Bloc were not allowed to participate in the Tour de France.

GREEN MOSCOW, STARTING FROM RED SQUARE
Twelve miles (20 km) along the Moskva

Start
Red Square

Finish
Red Square

⭐ Alexander Gardens
⭐ Statue of Peter the Great
⭐ Gorky Park

⭐ Neskuchny Garden
⭐ Luzhniki Olympic Complex
⭐ Sparrow Hills
(720 feet/220 m high)

⭐ Novodevichy Convent
⭐ Tolstoy's House
⭐ Cathedral of Christ the Savior

In full thaw *Moscow, Russia*

The collapse of the USSR happened only a quarter of a century ago. Muscovites' appetite for displaying their access to the brashest consumer goods remains fierce. A large car is still very much an object of desire. Since 2010, Moscow has been the most gridlocked city in the world. Cycling might be one solution, but change is slow. Still, the converts won't give up for anything, not even the harshest cold. In the winter of 2017, when temperatures reached record lows of 22°F (30°C) below zero, there were still nighttime processions by cycling activists. Appropriate infrastructure may be a long time coming, while the existing infrastructure is not very good, but Moscow's religious, architectural, and natural marvels are all accessible by bike without your feeling like you are risking your life. Only 3% of locals can benefit directly from the dedicated cycling space in the city center. The rest live too far away, often more than thirty minutes beyond the ring road. You can't bring your bike on the metro, Moscow's most efficient means of transport. The roads are often in poor condition, the pavements are too high, and the pedestrians inattentive. The drivers are sometimes careless, although relations between them and cyclists are beginning to thaw.

The popular *mamachari*

The *mamachari* is ubiquitous in Japan. Launched in the 1950s, this "mama's bike," with its sturdy U-shaped frame, was designed to carry young children, sometimes two or three of them at a time. People also use them for trips to the store or to go to the train station. A *mamachari* needs little maintenance and is of little interest to thieves. They're cheap too—around $120—although the more advanced ones with electric assistance are pricier.

THOUSANDS OF TEMPLES

17
temples
in the city are UNESCO
World Heritage Sites

1955
Year of the reconstruction
of the Kinkaku-ji, or Golden Pavilion,
the most famous

180
feet
(55m) the highest pagoda in Japan,
the To-ji (five floors)

50
million
visitors a year

京都市

Kyoto

2,000
temples in total in Kyoto:
around 1,600 Buddhist,
400 Shinto

Zen City *Kyoto, Japan*

When Kyoto was the imperial capital— as it was for more than a thousand years—one of its names was Heian-kyō, which means "capital of peace and tranquility." Little has changed on that score, at least in comparison with the hustle and bustle of Osaka and Kobe, its neighbors in a vast metropolitan area. With mostly flat terrain laid out in a grid, and asphalt that's as well maintained as the gravel of a Zen garden, Kyoto lends itself naturally to cycling. You might be surprised to know that in Kyoto you can ride on most of the sidewalks, which are shared with pedestrians, as long as you warn them of your presence with a gentle ring of your bell. The key thing to remember is that the Japanese drive on the left. Kyoto contains so many treasures of ancestral Japan. One of the loveliest routes is along a canal to the Philosopher's Walk, on which lie the temples of Ginkaku-ji (Temple of the Silver Pavilion) and Nanzen-ji. In April, hundreds of *sakura* (cherry trees) bloom. In fall, nature serves up other hues, particularly around the Katsura Imperial Villa farther west. Be sure to book a *ryokan* (type of traditional inn)—ideally, with a hot spring, or *onsen*.

A smartphone and you're off

It shouldn't surprise that the country of Samsung has been the first to develop a bike-share program in which you unlock your ride from a station using only your smartphone. It's called Ddareungi. The program's green-and-white bicycles have been in place in Seoul since 2015. Because South Korea is not a country to shy away from a challenge, 20,000 bikes have been promised by 2020. It will be a world record if they pull it off.

RIDE ALONG THE HAN
A gentle and flat 10-mile (16-km) cycle in Seoul, along the banks of the Han River

SEOUL

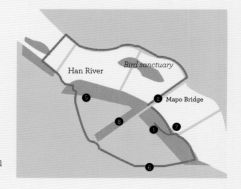

Han River
Bird sanctuary
Mapo Bridge

❶ Rent a bike at Yeouido Park
❷ Cross the Mapo Bridge to the north bank
❸ Jeoldu-san Martyrs' Shrine
❹ Seonyudo Park

❺ National Assembly
❻ Yeouido Saetgang Ecological Park
❼ Return the rental bike
❽ After returning your bike, finish with a stroll through Yeouido Park

Land of tranquil cycling *Seoul, South Korea*

Nightfall over the fifth-largest metropolitan area in the world by population (25.5 million)—behind Tokyo, Shanghai, Jakarta, and Delhi—is a stunning sight. Cool Seoul, connected Seoul, illuminated Seoul: where life is lived most intensely. By day, however, there are spots where you can find "the Land of the Morning Calm," thanks to the bicycle, which is a favored mode of transport here despite the pollution and the torrential summer rain. A "peaceful"

city that's pleasant to cycle has developed along the natural axis of the Han River, which flows into the Yellow Sea. Leisure time in Seoul is lived along the Han's wide curves and banks. From Gwangnaru Hangang Park in the east to Nanji Hangang Park in the west (where you can camp), more than 18 miles (30 km) of bike paths trace the line of the river. Be sure to return to Banpo Bridge for its unmissable rainbow-colored lighting display. Also

visit the *hanoks* (traditional houses) in Bukchon, the Changdeokgung Palace, or the more futuristic Dongdaemun Design Plaza farther north by juggling bike and subway. The cars of the latter are impressive, with heated seats, TV screens, and an impeccable Wi-Fi connection.

Beach Road, open to all

What's pleasant about the flat, smooth cycle path on Beach Road, which runs along the southeast side of Port Philip Bay, is that you pass sporty types in spandex and young dandies out shopping. In fact, it's the most popular cycling route in Melbourne. The return trip to Mordialloc is 28 miles (45 km) long. You can stop wherever you like; there are plenty of welcoming café terraces that offer sublime views across the bay.

THE WALL, AN ESSENTIAL AUSSIE CLIMB
Sportier cyclists should head for the Dandenong Ranges, east of Melbourne, to climb the Australian "Wall"

Duration
20 to 40min

Distance
3.8 miles
(6.1 km)

Difficulty
high

Gradient
average: 5%
maximum: 10%

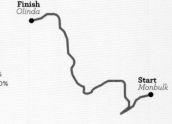

Finish
Olinda

Start
Monbulk

Cycle heaven *Melbourne, Australia*

The atmosphere at night is electric in the glare of the lights from Flinders Street Station by the Yarra River. By day, Melbourne puts on another face, with its wide avenues, a happy mix of contemporary and Victorian architectural styles, and a seemingly never-ending array of English-style parks and gardens. Melbourne has topped *The Economist's* ranking of "World's Most Livable Cities" for the past seven years (since 2011). It's quite

flat until it meets the slopes of the Dandenong Ranges to the north. Melbourne might very well be cycle heaven. As the most advanced Australian city, it is planning new cycle lanes on the major thoroughfares of Albert Street and Saint Kilda Road. The number of riders on this street dropped dramatically here in the 1990s—just when cycling was becoming huge elsewhere—because of a law obliging all cyclists to wear a helmet. Young

Melbourne professionals have ridden "fixies" for years, while women often prefer more "vintage" models with a basket attached to the handlebars. The Critical Mass ride is a friendly gathering that takes place on the last Friday of every month to great success. A study by Victoria University showed that four out of five cyclists were men, and that not even 10% were below thirty. So there's still some way to go.

157

The Whale Trail

Distances can be huge in Canada. Three hundred miles (500 km) beyond Montreal, the Saint Lawrence is already so wide you might mistake it for the sea, yet the river is still far from its mouth. As soon as the snow has melted on its north bank, you can happily pedal along the Véloroute des Baleines (Whale Trail) from Tadoussac to Baie-Comeau, a distance of 220 miles (350 km) over not-always-easy terrain. You'll see whales out on the water as you ride.

CYCLING IN CANADA!

1/3
of Quebecers cycle
at least once a week

17%
of journeys to work
in Ottawa are by
bicycle

37%
of cyclists in
Vancouver are
women

98
bicycle sales outlets
in Toronto

641 miles
(1,032 km)
of cycle paths and
lanes in Calgary

The Viking Trail *Newfoundland, Canada*

Newfoundland, at the mouth of the Saint Lawrence River, is as large as Iceland, but it's a part of Canada that tends to get overlooked. Life is tough here, and travel by bike can be a challenge. In addition to a determined mindset, you must properly gear up. Even in June or July—the ideal time for this trip—you should expect cold, violent winds, and even driving, icy rain. The Vikings discovered this land more than a thousand years ago, and so the

250 miles (400 km) of asphalt that run from St. Anthony in the northwest to Deer Lake have been dubbed the "Viking Trail." Highway 430, along which the Viking Trail runs, is initially a smooth stretch of road through a landscape of tundra, rocks, and lichens with caribou and moose. As it reaches the west coast, facing Labrador across the Strait of Belle Isle, the road veers south and the landscape changes. This second part of the route is much steeper but no

less rich, with such natural delights as the Arches Provincial Park, Western Brook Pond, and the cliffs of Gros Morne National Park. It's worth spending a few days here before reaching the relative comfort of Deer Lake. Newfoundland is a demanding but unique place to cycle.

A short tour of the Grand Canyon

The awesomely huge Grand Canyon in Colorado is a six-hour drive from Moab, which is farther south. At 277 miles (446 km) long, it boasts vertiginous steepness that cannot be cycled. You can, however, rent a bike for half a day in order to reach the Abyss, the famous cliff with a 4,900-foot (1,500 m) drop. Its forty geological strata depict the mineral history of the American continent. There's no question of descending the trails by mountain bike; they're for walkers only.

THREE DAYS ON THE WHITE RIM ROAD
To cycle the 70 miles (114 km) of this dirt road, book your camping spot in advance (six-month waiting list) and make sure that you're properly equipped:

an MTB

a gallon of water per person per day

a 4 x 4 for backup and water reserves

a helmet (obligatory)

The treasures of Moab *Canyonlands National Park, United States*

Utah, west of the Rockies, is a vast arena of geological curiosities. Monument Valley was popularized by the Westerns of old. Farther north, close to the little town of Moab—the "Mecca" of American mountain biking—Canyonlands National Park offers some unusual play areas for cyclists as long as you don't ride too fast. The White Rim Road is one option. It's a thrilling and memorable experience to cycle its 70 miles (114 km) through a unique

landscape in three or four days. But you can't just show up. You need a license to ride the road and another to camp there. You must rent a support vehicle to carry water supplies and take you to the Island in the Sky mesa, where the trek commences. Once you're onto the dirt trails, it's a fascinating decor of ocher earth, gray schist rock, and red sandstone with a temperature of around 86°F (30°C) at the height of summer. Then you reach the Lathrop

Canyon Trail and the approach to the remarkable Zeus and Moses buttes, followed by the steep hairpins of Shafer Canyon. The White Rim Road was constructed in 1950 to access uranium deposits that turned out to be disappointing. The wealth was elsewhere—under the open sky.

Thrills on Chacaltaya

Mount Chacaltaya has lost its grandeur. Global warming ensured the disappearance of its glacier and its ski resort, which was located virtually at its summit (17,785 feet / 5,421 m). All that remains is the road from La Paz, 19 miles (30 km) away. The ideal direction to cycle the road is downhill, descending 6,500 feet (2,000 m) to Lake Titicaca through a lunar landscape that is more desertic than rocky. A rare experience.

ON THE SHORES OF LAKE TITICACA
From La Paz to Puno, a six-day trek over the heights, from Bolivia to Peru

- La Paz, **11,800 feet** > Tiquina, **12,500 feet**
- Tiquina > Copacabana, **12,600 feet**
- Copacabana > Isla del Sol, **13,360 feet**
- Isla del Sol > Ilave, **11,680 feet**
- Ilave > Plateria, **12,560 feet**
- Plateria > Puno, **12,555 feet**

Duration
6 to 10 days

Distance
217 miles
(350 km)

Difficulty
high, owing to
the altitude

Gear
winter clothing
The warmest month is
November: 55°F (13°C)
average

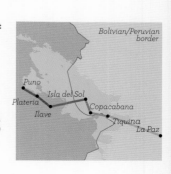

The first Inca *Lake Titicaca, Bolivia and Peru*

The waters of Lake Titicaca are of a fascinatingly deep blue. Unfortunately, it is not possible to make a full circuit (870 miles/1,400 km) of the highest navigable lake in the world. There are too many poor-quality trails on the northern shore, and no administrative border between Peru and Bolivia. It's better to enjoy the grandiose spectacle of the Andes from the southern shore. You can rent perfectly suitable bicycles for bikepacking in La Paz and then acclimatize at altitude—11,942 feet (3,640 m)—which is essential. Maybe start with a trip higher up the Altiplano (high plateau) to 13,450 feet (4,100 m) by bus or by hitchhiking (the road traffic is awful). From Sorata, you climb just as high before descending toward the lake. The landscape is stunning, and the locals are very friendly. After the waterside resort of Copacabana, a detour to the Yampupata Peninsula is a must, followed by Isla del Sol (Island of the Sun). In the Peruvian territory, the culture shock and riot of colors is just as intense. Plateria is a jewel. This high-altitude trek is the discovery of another world. Our trip ends in Puno (100,000 inhabitants), where Viracocha, the creator-deity in Incan mythology, supposedly brought forth Manco Capac, the first Inca, from the waters of Lake Titicaca.

On the moon, down in the valley

The expanses of white salts, the red or green lakes, the weirdly shaped rocks, and the trails overlooked by the volcanoes are a bit farther away, as are the herds of llamas and the flocks of pink flamingos. But just outside San Pedro, you can encounter the extraordinary in a single day. The Valley of the Moon is an initiatory trip to these lands, through the gravel and the sand, beneath a burning sun.

77°F
(25°C)
Maximum temperature, in January

32°F
(0°C)
During the summer nights

267 miles
(430 km)
Circumference of the Salar de Uyuni

7,998 fee
(2,438 m)
Altitude of San Pedro de Atacama

Extreme territories *San Pedro de Atacama, Chile*

This place lies at the same latitude as balmy Rio de Janeiro, but on the other side of South America, in the highly arid foothills of the Altiplano, 186 miles (300 km) from the Pacific coast. The village-oasis of San Pedro de Atacama (5,000 inhabitants living in remote austerity) is the starting point for some great adventures. The Atacama Desert to the south is the first option, taking three or four days. In the heart of it, you will come across the first *salar* (salt flat)

in this vast region straddling the borderlands of Chile, Bolivia, and Argentina. True adventurers—those who don't suffer from *soroche* (altitude sickness)—should head north, passing through the huge geyser site of El Tatio. After crossing a mountain pass (at nearly 16,400 feet/5,000 m) on the slopes of the volcano Ollagüe, you ride down into Bolivia. Then cycle along the trails of Sud Lípez toward one of the most astounding landscapes on the

face of the planet: the Salar d'Uyuni, which is so vast that when you stand on it, you can never see its edge. It contains one-third of the world's reserves of lithium (a mineral used to make certain electric batteries). Allow at least six days to return to San Pedro. The memory of nature's extremes will stay with you forever.

France's vineyards

If cycling along the Loire River offers access to some famous vineyards, the same goes for the other major French wine-producing regions. The 25-mile (40 km) Voie des Vignes from Beaune to Nolay in Burgundy takes in Meursault, Puligny-Montrachet, and Santenay. Meanwhile, the Entre-deux-Mers cycle path in the Bordeaux region crosses Margaux, Moulis, Saint-Estèphe, and Médoc. If the Rhône wines are more to your taste, then ride the ViaRhôna by way of Condrieu, Côte-Rôtie, and Châteauneuf-du-Pape. Cheers!

CHÂTEAU VALLEY
Explore the Loire Valley for 300 miles (500 km)

1 Saumur
2 Ussé
3 Langeais

4 Azay-le-Rideau
5 Villandry
6 Chenonceau

7 Amboise
8 Cheverny
9 Blois

10 Chambord
11 Sully-sur-Loirev

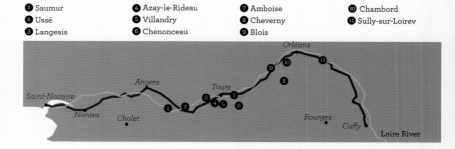

Châteaux and vineyards *Loire Valley, France*

France is an exceptional country for all forms of cycling—touring included. And its longest river, the Loire, is perfectly suited to this. Its banks mark the start of the EuroVelo 6 trail, which traverses the heart of the Old Continent to the Romanian coast, on the Black Sea. At 370 miles (600 km), La Loire à Vélo is a rather shorter itinerary. It is quite flat, with the exception of a few limestone hills that commence beside the Atlantic Ocean. Nearly a million cyclists ride it each year. The Val de Loire section is the most attractive and enriching. One hundred and seventy miles (280 km) long, it starts at Chalonnes-sur-Loire, west of Angers, and ends at Sully-sur-Loire, east of Orléans. It is recommended to ride from west to east to take advantage of the prevailing winds. The trip should take 12/13 days, with no shortage of places to eat and sleep. Pedal at your own pace, and enjoy the bountiful river landscape dotted with splendid Renaissance châteaux. Indulge in the pleasures of the local gastronomy—from pike perch to the famous Crottin de Chavignol goat cheese—and, of course, the many fine wines along the way.

Pedal after a monster

The legend (or hoax) of the Loch Ness Monster is nearly a century old, but it is still just as popular. The Inverness municipality has been promoting cycling as a way to reach the 22.5-mile (36 km) long freshwater loch rather than adding to the motor traffic on the A82 road. You reach the south bank of Loch Ness via Dores, then turn back whenever you like—such as when you've tired of waiting for Nessie to appear.

THE HEBRIDES ARCHIPELAGOS

500
islands and islets

44,600
inhabitants

3
runways at Barra Airport, where the regularly scheduled flights land on the beach

2,800 sq. mi.
(7,200 km²)
total area of the islands (twice that of Long Island)

5
hours by ferry from Oban (on the Scottish mainland)

Scotland in the open air *Outer Hebrides, United Kingdom*

A week between May and October is perfect—just the time that you need to unhurriedly explore the Outer Hebrides in northwest Scotland, from the southernmost inhabited island, Vatersay, to the Butt of Lewis Lighthouse in the very north, where you can glimpse dolphins that are drawn by the mildness of the Gulf Stream. The road is not always flat, particularly toward the end of the itinerary. Sometimes you'll take a ferry from one island to another: Lochboisdale to Barra, to start with, then to Eriskay, and finally from Berneray to Harris. The journey is one of surprises, wonders, and excuses to stop for a break. It's a wild landscape with thatched houses and Shetland ponies. The old stone and ferns are dark in color, but the sand of the beaches on North Uist and at Luskentyre is luminous white, contrasting with the turquoise of the sea. Short stages of 6 to 35 miles (10 to 60 km) are recommended, with nights in a bed-and-breakfast. The Hebrides have a long history, as evidenced by the Callanish Stones, an arrangement of Neolithic standing stones on the Isle of Lewis. It is, indeed, a privilege to cycle here.

Right across Europe

The EuroVelo 6 is 2,269 miles (3,653 km) long and
crosses ten countries from France to Romania. It is
the most popular of the seventeen EuroVelo cycle
routes that traverse the continent. No. 2, for example,
links the west coast of Ireland to Moscow via Berlin,
whereas No. 13 gives a nod to the Cold War, following
the line of the Iron Curtain from the northern reaches
of Scandinavia to the south of the former Yugoslavia.

CROSS EUROPE BY BIKE
The EuroVelo 6, from the banks of the Loire (France) to Constanța (Romania)

2,269 miles
(3,653 km)
officially but some
routes can reach 3,100
miles (5,000 km)

10 countries crossed

35 to 45 miles/day on average
(60 to 75 km)

6 major European rivers

The romantic Danube
Passau, Germany, to Vienna, Austria

The Donauradweg ("Danube Cycle Path" in German) is the loveliest and most ridden section of the EuroVelo 6. May to June is the best time for this escapade, lasting a good week and 211 miles (340 km), especially if you wish to ride as a couple. The weather is pleasant, but the organized groups aren't out in force yet. The popularity of the Donauradweg is due to its romantic setting, through which Europe's most significant river flows. It leads to an exceptional capital city, Vienna, which is full of historic and cultural riches, contemporary energy, and many beautiful parks. Technically, the trip starts in Germany, but Passau is a border town, so you're immediately in Austria. From there on, let yourself be drawn by the beauty of the river. At Schlögen, a meander gives it the appearance of a hairpin bend in the mountains, with spectacular views. A little farther on, after Linz, where Mozart composed his Symphony No. 36, the Danube becomes narrower and more turbulent, with hills and forests on either side. Melk and its Benedictine abbey, and the vineyards of the Wachau, follow. The most majestic part is to come, when the Danube widens into the Tulln Basin before shrinking again as it enters the Viennese Woods. The Austrian Danube is a dream—one that should be shared.

In Olympic form

Our Greek itinerary ignores the plain of Marathon, which is located northeast of Athens. The route of the road cycling event of the first modern Olympics, in 1896, involved a 54-mile (87 km) ride from the capital to Marathon and back. The winner was a Greek, Aristidis Konstantinidis, with an average speed of 16 mph (26 km/h). The twenty-year-old Frenchman Paul Masson was the king of the Neo Phaliron Velodrome in Athens, taking three gold medals.

CRETE, THE OTHER GREECE
Sublime coasts and superb highlands

When?
May, June, or
September

15
days to complete a
circuit of the island—
more than 620 miles
(1,000 km)

Eat
the Cretan diet: fruit,
legumes, cereals, olive
oil, grilled fish

3,280 feet
(1,000 m)
and more of climbing
each day

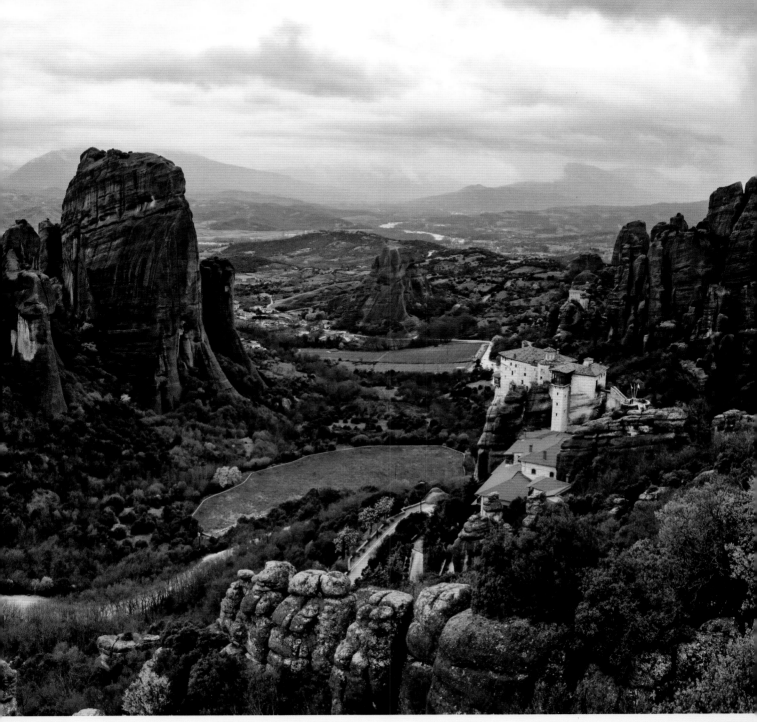

Apollo and monasteries   *Athens to the Meteora, Greece*

The Greek islands—particularly the Cyclades—have always tempted travelers the most, but the Meteora and its monasteries 250 miles (400 km) north of Athens also hold a promise of history and heritage—with plenty of climbing. The Greek highlands are demanding in their own way. Ten days is a decent amount of time to allow for a visit. You can either camp out or sleep with a roof over your head, or alternate between the two. Ride out of Athens via

Mandra to the west, then Thebes and Vagia. The Attica road then leads to the foot of Mount Helicon (literally, "the tortuous mountain"), which rises to 5,738 feet (1,748 m). You climb to nearly 3,280 feet (1,000 m) toward Kyriaki, then the wonders commence: the ancient site of Delphi and Mount Parnassus, which, like Mount Helicon, is considered to be sacred to Apollo. Then head north in the direction of the Plain of Thessaly via Xatzipetros, the

highest peak of Mount Koziakas, at 6,236 feet (1,901 m). Stop at Kalabaka before devoting a couple of days to the "hanging" monasteries of the Meteora. Orthodox Christian monks built these in the Middle Ages upon impressive gray rocks created by erosion. Six of the original twenty-four are open to visitors, including the Great Meteoron. The rest are in ruin. The steps up to the Great Meteoron are a century old. This final climb is the loveliest of all.

St. Moritz base camp

The elegant winter resort of St. Moritz in eastern
Switzerland becomes a marvelous base camp for
cyclists in summer. One of the most beautiful trails,
which never descends lower than 4,900 feet (1,500 m),
heads north into the Swiss National Park, where you
can see chamois and ibex, before skirting Lago di
Livigno in Italy, and then, after 68 miles (110 km), returns
via the Livigno Pass, at 7,595 feet (2,318 m), and the
Bernina Pass at 7,638 feet (2,328 m). Divine!

SEVEN DAYS IN REVERSE
A trip to the source of the Rhône

- Geneva > Morges, 36 miles (58 km), 1,300 feet (400 m) of altitude gain
- Morges > Montreux, 26 miles (42 km), 1,300 feet (400 m) of altitude gain
- Montreux > Martigny, 29 miles (47 km), 525 feet (160 m) of altitude gain
- Martigny > Sierre, 28.5 miles (46 km), 328 feet (100 m) of altitude gain
- Sierre > Brigue, 26 miles (42 km), 850 feet (260 m) of altitude gain
- Brigue > Oberwald, 31 miles (50 km), 3,280 feet (1,000 m) of altitude gain
- Oberwald > Andermatt, 23.5 miles (38 km) via the Furka Pass,
  3,600 feet (1,100 m) of altitude gain, 3,280 feet (1,000 m) of altitude loss

Duration
7 days

Distance
205 miles
(330 km)

Difficulty
medium to
high

Tip
mountain gears

The finest "Côtes du Rhône" *ViaRhôna, Switzerland*

"Côtes du Rhône" may be a famous French wine region, but the finest "Rhône Hills" (as the name means in English) are to be found in Switzerland. Here in the Valais region, the roads snake uphill beside the mountain pastures overlooking the Rhône River, the first 190 miles (300 km) of which flow through Switzerland. To follow it upstream is an excuse for a wonderful trip—a most relaxing ride—starting in Geneva and finishing with an assault on

the glacier from where the river flows. A hybrid bike is recommended because around 30 miles (50 km) of the ViaRhôna—also ridden in summer, even in reverse—is along dirt trails. A week is a pleasant time frame in which to enjoy the light reflecting off Lake Geneva; the approach to Mont Blanc at Martigny; the castles, orchards, and vineyards of Sierre; the "untamable" Rhône at Loèche; and the pines of the Conches Valley, where the river takes the name

"Rotten" (in the local Swiss German dialect). The final day is a sporty one, with a climb of 3,600 feet (1,100 m) amid a landscape of rock and ice to the Furka Pass at 7,969 feet (2,429 m). A couple of miles from the top, you step off the bike on a right-hand hairpin bend, opposite the Hotel Belvedere, and walk to the icy cave shrouded in a magical blue light, the beating heart of the Rhône.

The North of *Game of Thrones*

Game of Thrones, the most streamed TV series in the world, wasn't shot only in the American studios of HBO. Its emblematic locations (Dothraki Sea, Winterfell, Vale of Arryn) can be cycled for real in Ireland, 300 miles (500 km) above Kerry. There are forests, lakes, spectacular slopes, magnificent coasts, and numerous medieval castles, making the "real" land of *Game of Thrones*, between Belfast and Londonderry, a lovely place to explore by bike.

IRISH WEEKEND
Three days of wonder on the Ring of Kerry

- **Day 1:** Killarney > Cahersiveen via Killorglin and Glenbeigh (45 miles/70 km)
- **Day 2:** Cahersiveen > Sneem via Waterville and Caherdaniel (30 miles/50 km)
- **Day 3:** Sneem > Killarney, via Kenmare (30 miles/50 km)

Duration
3 days

Distance
105 miles
(170 km)

Difficulty
easy

Gear
road bike and
rain jacket

Sublime and wild *County Kerry, Ireland*

The surprising beauty of the Emerald Isle lies in the never-ending contrasts of its landscapes. Ireland is a choice destination for cycling. In addition to giant rocks, wild horses grazing beside lakes, an ever-present sense of mythology, and good cheer in every pub, there are also some fantastic routes. While some are quite demanding, others, such as the 105 mile (170 km) long Ring of Kerry in the southwest, are gentler. County

Kerry is a tourist classic with a beautiful Atlantic coast and stunning landscapes in the interior. A long weekend is ideal to take it all in. The charming and colorful Killarney is the starting (and finishing) point from where you'll explore the wild Atlantic coast. The views over Macgillycuddy's Reeks, a mountain range containing the island's highest peak (Carrauntoohil), are sumptuous, and the discovery of Cahersiveen, a ravishing fishing port, is idyllic. The

second day includes Caherdaniel and its golden beach and ends at Sneem, where they fish for crab. The final day covers Kenmare. This Celtic itinerary will leave you with a long, lingering taste of salt and wind—and Guinness, of course!

Strade bianche, in Tuscany

Tuscany's old white gravel roads ("*strade bianchi*" in Italian) give their name to a top-flight race that takes cycling back to another era, when racing cyclists had to compete, unsupported, over distances that make the more arduous stages in today's Grand Tours seem like walks in the park. It was another race over these same roads and hills, the Eroica, which was created twenty years ago, that started the trend of "vintage" cycling.

● **Day 1:** Sienna > Radda in Chianti (25 miles/40 km)

● **Day 2:** Radda in Chianti > Greve in Chianti (25 miles/40 km)

● **Day 3:** Greve in Chianti > Florence (25 miles/40 km)

● **Day 4:** Florence > Colle di Val d'Elsa via Tavernelle (50 miles /80 km)

● **Day 5:** Colle di Val d'Elsa > Sienna (25 miles/40 km)

Duration
5 days

Distance
around 155 miles
(250 km) in total

Difficulty
average

Gear
mountain
bike advisable

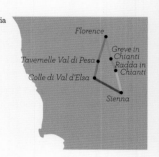

Florence

Greve in
Chianti
Radda in
Chianti

Tavernelle Val di Pesa

Colle di Val d'Elsa

Sienna

Breakaway in Chianti *Sienna to Florence, Italy*

Chianti, which lies in Tuscany between Sienna and Florence, has been a wine region since antiquity. Magnificently undulating, Chianti's varied soil and climate help to produce some of the most prestigious wines in Italy, if not the world. It is also cycling country, and the wine route is a must. It traverses the countryside for several days, past vine-covered hillsides, olive plantations lined with cypress trees, impossibly charming villages, and towns with a seemingly endless cultural heritage. It's a tranquil adventure that involves a moderate amount of physical exercise compensated by the pleasure of the surroundings. After Sienna and its many fine attractions—not least of which is the historic Piazza del Campo—comes the discovery of Radda in Chianti, followed by Greve in Chianti, and the chance to sample some fabulous vintages. Then Florence, cradle of the Renaissance, with enough architectural sights and museums to keep you occupied for weeks. But it's back on the road— direction: Colle di Val d'Elsa, renowned for its crystal glassware—by way of Tavernelle, a former stopping point on the Via Francigena, an ancient pilgrim route from Canterbury to Rome, before carrying on back to Sienna. Tuscany by bike is a wonderful waking dream.

Can you make it to Montenegro?

Once you reach Dubrovnik, you will be tempted to just keep on riding. Sixty miles (100 km) farther down the coast, you reach Kotor in Montenegro. The bay is as beautiful as a Norwegian fjord. A climb of 4,900 feet (1,500 m) in 27 hairpin bends gets you to the top of the impressive rocky wall that overlooks the town. Then you enter the Lovćen National Park, named after the eponymous dark rocky mountain that gave its name to the country—which is half as big as Belgium. Now you may commence an unforgettable week's cycling in Montenegro.

SPLIT TO DUBROVNIK VIA THE ISLANDS

Start in **Split** ❶ > ferry to **Brač** ❷ > 37-mile (60 km) cycle around Brač > ferry to Split > ferry to **Hvar** ❸ > 50-mile (80 km) cycle around Hvar > ferry to **Korčula** ❹ > 25-mile (40 km) cycle around Korčula > ferry to **Pelješac** peninsula ❺ > 75-mile (120 km) cycle to **Dubrovnik** ❻

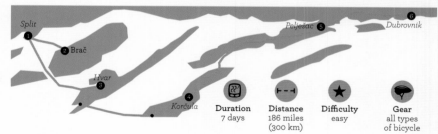

Duration	Distance	Difficulty	Gear
7 days	186 miles (300 km)	easy	all types of bicycle

Dalmatian pearls *Split to Dubrovnik, Croatia*

Barely 125 miles (200 km) separate Split from Dubrovnik via the coast. It's a magnificent road. You pedal between limestone cliffs and pines on the left, and the turquoise water of the Adriatic on the right. The weather should be perfect, unless the bora wind is blowing. The shores of Dalmatia are not far from some of the most sumptuous offerings of the Mediterranean basin. To discover some even more beautiful landscapes, you need to cycle inland a few miles. As for the Dalmatian islands across the water, Brač, the first one, opposite Split, is just a foretaste. You take the ferry over—the first of five that you'll be taking this week. May and October are the ideal months to visit, both in terms of the weather (not too hot) and there being fewer tourists than at the height of summer. The second island, Hvar, is considered to be one of the most beautiful in the world. You cycle between sea and hills, and among fields of lavender, olive trees, and vineyards. Next comes Korčula, with the Biokovo range facing you over on the mainland. Then it's the Pelješac Peninsula and the vineyards where they grow *plavac mali*, the most common grape variety in Croatia. Some white wines are excellent too. Dubrovnik is not that far away now, but once you reach it, who's to say if you'll still think this picturesque city remains the most brilliant of all the Dalmatian pearls.

181

The mystical Westfjords

If you're looking for a more original approach to
Iceland, look no further than the Westfjords. Leave
Route 1 for Route 60 or 68 after Staður, then the 61.
They're not always the best-maintained roads and
can sometimes turn into rutted trails. The sky is low.
It rains even more than elsewhere, and dwellings are
few and far between. There is, however, a mystical
feel to the place. The Westfjords are a particularly
intense experience, as if the edge of the land were
truly the edge of the world.

ROUTE 1: 840 MILES (1,350 KM)
A tour of Iceland via the main road,
which is accessible to all types of car.
Turn off to the Westfjords between
Borgarnes and Blönduós

Vatnajökulsþjóðgarður

1 Reykjavík, vibrant, colorful capital
2 Borgarnes, toward the Westfjords
3 Blönduós, across the Tröllaskagi peninsula
4 Akureyri, for whale watching
5 Egilsstaðir, toward the East Fjords
6 Höfn, not far from the glaciers
7 Selfoss, and its famous waterfalls

An unforgettable odyssey *Iceland*

You'll be lucky if the temperature reaches 50°F (10°C) in summer. The howling westerly winds blow so hard that they can reduce a cyclist's average speed to below 6 mph (10 km/h). The rain seems never-ending, the mist unshakable. In June and July—the most favorable months—the midnight sun encourages you to never stop riding, but you'll slip from the saddle eventually, drunk with fatigue and covered with mud or dust. A cycle trip in Iceland is more than an adventure—it's an expedition. It is a unique experience, nourished by the feeling of having set foot on another planet. What wild beauty, what emotions, what memories! There is nothing banal about making the full circuit of Iceland on Route 1—clockwise so as to minimize the effect of the contrary winds. Those 840 miles (1,350 km), starting from Reykjavík, are rarely flat, but they make for an unforgettable odyssey through a natural landscape unlike any other—a geography of fjords, volcanoes, glaciers, and geysers. You'll never forget the blue of the sea, particularly the stretch between Höfn and Selfoss in the southeast, the light from the Jökulsárlón glacial lagoon, the breathtaking Fjaðrárgljúfur canyon, and the majesty of the Eyjafjallajökull glacier. Upon returning to Reykjavík, you'll find the warm waters of the Blue Lagoon—although something of a cliché—will feel extra special.

Riders vs. Wild

As paradisiacal as the Emerald Isle appears, parts of its challenging topography have inspired an extreme cycling event: the Rumble in the Jungle, named after the epic boxing match between Mohammed Ali and George Foreman. It takes place over four days each June, and sees competitors race between Negombo, Haputale, and Kandy, combating hot, humid jungle, mud, wetlands, and hostile vegetation. You'll see wild elephants, leopards, and snakes. It's like *Man vs. Wild*, but with a mountain bike!

THE TREASURES OF SRI LANKA

From Colombo, the capital, to Matara in the far south, it's a trip of more than 430 miles (700 km), so it's worth taking your time.

- Colombo > Anuradhapura via Negombo (93 miles/150 km)
- Anuradhapura > Dambulla (51.5 miles)
- Dambulla > Matale (37 miles/60 km)
- Matale > Kandy (30 miles/50 km)
- Kandy > Adam's Peak (62 miles/100 km)
- Adam's Peak > Ratnapura, 93 miles/150 km)
- Ratnapura > Matara (80 miles/130 km)

Duration
15 days

Difficulty
average

Climbing
around
26,250 feet
(8,000 m)

Tip
January to March
Start early, around 6 a.m.
Drink 1.3 gallons (6 l)
of water a day

The Emerald Isle *Colombo to Matara, Sri Lanka*

Spice and colors are the themes for a bicycle adventure in Sri Lanka. The island is known as the "Teardrop of India," but it's a land of smiles as the country continues to rebuild following the terrible tsunami of 2004, which ravaged 500 miles (800 km) of coast and took more than 35,000 lives. Sri Lanka boasts so many riches: tea plantations stretching as far as the eye can see, temples of absolute tranquility, luxuriant highland landscapes, sublime beaches, and large elephants galore. However, you must take a few precautions: drink more than you think you need (there is an abundance of spring water and coconuts) and watch out for the thieving monkeys! Get used to the slow drivers on the left-hand side of the road. Leave Colombo, the infernal capital, as fast as you can. Take a fortnight (at the very least) and let the roads and trails unfold like a magic carpet ride, visiting the historic town of Anuradhapura in the north, Kaudulla National Park, Dambulla, the ocher rock fortress of Sigiriya and its royal parks, the spice gardens of Matale, delightful Kandy, and the 4,500 steps to the top of Adam's Peak. Elephants are everywhere, as far down as Matara and its lovely beaches at the island's southern tip. Yes, they too sometimes bathe in the Indian Ocean.

Mayotte, a secret in the Indian Ocean

There is no shortage of surprising islands around Madagascar to cycle, but Mayotte, to the north, is the most unexpected. This French department that is only three times the size of Paris, with its highest point Mount Benara at 2,170 feet (660 m), is a wonderful place for cycle trekking. You'll ride amid fruit plantations, see zebus, experience the mangrove, and glimpse humpback whales out at sea. A week here is a joy.

RIDE THE NATIONALE 7
This famous road snakes across the "Red Island"—with its mix of Asian and African cultures—from Antananarivo to Toliara

620 miles
(1,000 km)
distance

15 days
riding

★

Difficulty
average

Season
June, September,
October

The baobab road *Antananarivo to Toliara, Madagascar*

Exploring Madagascar by bike is enchanting. The culturally mixed "Red Island" reveals itself as you pass through an extremely wide variety of landscapes. And the local people are very friendly indeed. The native fauna and flora add to the enjoyment, with the landscapes of paddy fields, the red earth of Africa, and the echoes of lost paradises. The 620-mile (1,000 km) ride south along the Nationale 7 from Antananarivo to Toliara is similar to that of a backcountry road. The poverty that is all too real in Madagascar means there are relatively few cars. You'll soon leave Antananarivo and its 12 sacred hills behind. Charming, joyful Antsirabe, which is renowned for its craftspeople, is the gateway to a landscape of volcanoes and wild lakes. Fianarantsoa has vineyards and tea plantations. You can also get away from the Nationale 7 and take the train to Manakara and the beautiful coast, or visit Ilakaka and its sapphire mines, with the Andringitra Massif—the Madagascan highlands—as a backdrop. As you approach Toliara, you'll find the trail is lined with baobabs, those ever-surprising giant trees. At the end of the road, beside the Mozambique Channel, on the Tropic of Capricorn, you'll find an unforgettable night sky.

Pedal in Zanzibar

Tanzania is also on the Indian Ocean. It has lagoons, coconut trees, and coral reefs. What's the best way to discover Unguja, the principal island in the Zanzibar archipelago? By bike! There are lots of organized tours and bike rental places in Zanzibar City. As you head toward Nungwi in the north, and its sublime beach—a distance of 60 miles (100 km) there and back—you'll cross the Koani hills with their caves, then the luxuriant Kichwele Forest, before a well-earned nap on the seashore.

HEART OF AFRICA
From Mbeya to Mwanza, a trek through Tanzania on roads and tracks

- Mbeya > Sumbawanga (260 miles/420 km)
- Sumbawanga > Katavi National Park (115 miles /184 km)
- Katavi National Park > Kigoma (205 miles/330 km)
- Kigoma > Moyowosi and Kigosi Game Reserves (112 miles/180 km)
- Kigosi Game Reserve > Shinyanga (143 miles/230 km)
- Shinyanga > Mwanza (95 miles/152 km)

Duration
at least
14 days

Distance
around
913 miles
(1,470 km)

Difficulty
medium to high

Accommodation
lodges or under
canvas

Tip
1 gallon (4.5 l)
of drinking
water per stage

The most beautiful safari *Mbeya to Mwanza, Tanzania*

Tanzania is a prime destination for safaris because it offers one of the greatest concentrations of wild animals in the world. It also offers some wonderful cycling. You can explore Tanzania and its sumptuous nature from south to north over approximately 600 miles (1,000 km) of roads and tracks in good condition. It is an unforgettable odyssey. Start from Mbeya, not far from the Zambian border, on a fertile plateau at an altitude

of 5,570 feet (1,700 m) where they grow an abundance of tobacco, rice, and bananas. The route runs parallel to the Great Rift Valley. You'll cross the Katavi National Park, which is known for its crocodiles and hippopotamuses. It is less popular than other parks, but not to be missed. Then travel to Lake Tanganyika, which forms the border with the Democratic Republic of the Congo, until Kigoma and the frontier with Burundi. Next comes the

Moyowosi and Kigosi Game Reserves that precede Shinyanga and its diamond mines. The adventure comes to an end in Mwanza, the port city on Lake Victoria, which is the largest lake in Africa. This trek through grassy savannah, light-filled forests, and wide expanses full of baobabs promises to be an enduring souvenir, made all the sweeter by the friendly Tanzanians themselves.

North to the mountains

The far north of Vietnam, close to the Chinese border, is quite mountainous in stark contrast to the flatness of the Mekong Delta. There is no shortage of climbs around Sa Pa, a charming tourist town built during the time of French colonization. The loveliest of them will take you to the Tram Ton Pass, at an altitude of 6,233 feet (1,900 m), before you descend out of the cold and fog toward the sun and light of the luxuriant Lai Chau Valley.

BETWEEN THE ARMS OF THE MEKONG
The mystery and beauty of the Mekong, from Ho Chi Minh City to Phnom Penh—four days in Vietnam and one in Cambodia

● **Day 1:** Ho Chi Minh-Ville > Bên Tre (37 miles/60 km)
● **Day 2:** Bên Tre > Can Tho (37 miles/60 km)
● **Day 3:** Can Tho > Cao Lanh (31 miles/50 km)
● **Day 4:** Cao Lanh > Chau Doc (31 miles/50 km)
● **Day 5:** Chau Doc > Phnom Penh (50 miles/80 km)

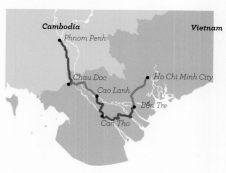

Duration
5 days

Distance
186 miles
(300 km)

Difficulty
humid heat

Tour of the Nine Dragons *Mekong Delta, Vietnam and Cambodia*

The waters of the Mekong are neither emerald nor turquoise, but instead earthy. In the novel *The Lover,* Marguerite Duras underscores the strange attraction the Mekong holds: "Never, in my entire life, will I see rivers of such beauty, grandeur, and wildness as the arms of the Mekong." The Mekong Delta in the far south of Vietnam, just beneath its Cambodian neighbor, offers unique, half-aquatic landscapes. This vast plain traversed by the river's nine arms—locally called "Nine Dragons"—is both the breadbasket of Southeast Asia (40% of the world's rice is grown here) and a land endlessly threatened by floods and tides as capricious as they are fertile. Cycling here in winter, when the temperature drops to a less stifling 85°F (30°C), mostly over tracks and trails rather than on asphalt, is a fabulous experience. Make it a five-day ride from Ho Chi Minh City—formerly known as Saigon—to Phnom Penh, the capital of Cambodia. It is a pleasant trip, full of lovely surprises: the verdant canals of Bến Tre; the floating market of Cái Răng; the plantations of jackfruit, durian, papaya, and mango of Châu Đốc; and the people of the Mekong themselves, who are at ease on the water as we are on the road.

The legend of the M41

It's called the "Cloud Road," or the Pamir Highway, after the mountains that it traverses west of the Himalayas. It comes from Afghanistan, skirts Pakistan, and runs right up to the north of Kyrgyzstan, sometimes at altitudes of 10,000 to 13,000 feet (3,000 to 4,000 m). Part of the Silk Road in centuries past, it is now used heavily by Chinese truckers taking their time. One is always at the mercy of rock falls, landslides, and the eternal snow. The M41 is also an emblematic route for long-haul cycle tourists.

THE HEIGHTS OF KYRGYZSTAN
Five places to explore on foot or by bike in this extremely beautiful country, with all the challenges of altitude and badly surfaced roads

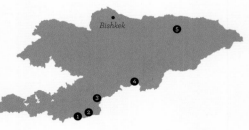

❶ **Lenin Peak,** the second-highest summit in Kyrgyzstan, 23,406 feet (7,134 m)

❷ **Kyzylart Pass,** on the border with Tajikistan, on the M41, 14,042 feet (4,280 m)

❸ **Terek Pass,** off the M41, in the south of the Osh region, 12,172 feet (4,131 m)

❹ **Torugart Pass,** on the Chinese border, 12,310 feet (3,752 m)

❺ **Issyk-Kul Lake,** the largest in the country—111 miles (178 km) long, 37 miles (60 km) wide—5,272 feet (1,607 m)

Beyond the Pamirs *Song Kol Lake, Kyrgyzstan*

You come across few people in this mountainous landscape, a place quite unimaginable if you've never cycled there. A few livestock farmers round their yurts, which are potential places to sleep for the tired traveler. You'll see herds of horses, sheep, and yaks in the *jailoo* (summer pasture), the fat grass of a Kyrgyz summer. There is not a tree to be seen on these high plains of Central Asia. Noisy marmots warn their brethren of human approach, then quickly return to their burrow. If you want to explore the mountains of Kyrgyzstan, the most impoverished of the former Soviet republics, you should forget the Pamirs in the south and turn off the M41 at Suusamyr, before Osh. Soon you'll have to climb the Kalmak-Ashu Pass, an ascent of 5,570 feet (1,700 m), often pushing your bike on a bad road with a surface like corrugated sheet metal. At 11,300 feet (3,446 m), you'll begin the descent toward Song Kol Lake—a marvel with very clear waters. Watch out for the wolves and leopards that prowl about sometimes. The largest natural reserve of fresh water in Kyrgyzstan is a magnificent destination to explore in its own right. Kyrgyzstan is an adventure, indeed.

193

One mountain, five peaks

It is possible to get a little bored of tropical Hainan, but if you're in the south of the island, just head inland to Wuzhishan at 2,600 feet (800 m). The landscape becomes mountainous and quite different. Five peaks soar from one of the world's few remaining natural tropical forests. This is Wǔzhǐ Shān (literally, "Five Finger Mountain"); its highest peak attains 6,040 feet (1,840 m). It is impossible to get near it by bike; the only options are hiking or rafting.

THE HAWAII OF THE EAST
Explore the wonders of Hainan: the coconut palms of Dadonghai, the hot springs and coffee plantations of Xinglong, the pepper and vanilla gardens of Banqiao

- Haikou > Qinglan
- Qinglan > Qionghai
- Qionghai > Wanning
- Wanning > Yalong Bay
- Yalong Bay > Sanya

- Sanya > Banqiao
- Banqiao > Changjiang
- Changjiang > Danzhou
- Danzhou > Haikou

 Duration
9 to 10 days

 Distance
560 to 620 miles (900 to 1,000 km)

 Difficulty
medium, 80% flat roads

 Gear
hybrid bike—gravel type, 10% trails

Around the Dragon's Tail *Hainan Island, China*

Hainan Island is not merely a spaceport for Chinese satellite launches, but also a place of tropical beauty and enchantment. It's the southernmost point of the People's Republic, 300 miles (500 km) southwest of Hong Kong and closer still to Vietnam. The "Tail of the Dragon," as Hainan is nicknamed, has many delights to offer, with its shoreline, mountains, and plains; and its luxuriant nature, with rice paddies, fields of sugarcane and sweet

potatoes, and banana and pineapple plantations. It also provides the setting for a magical ten-day cycle tour. Most of the urban areas of Hainan, which is comparable in size to Taiwan and Belgium, lie along the South China Sea coast, but there are many protected trails—both asphalt and small cobblestones. Start out from Haikou, the capital of the northern province (two million inhabitants), and progress clockwise along the coast for nearly

620 miles (1,000 km) at a fair speed. The wind is never your foe, because it helps you to bear the humidity, while the mountains are but a vision. It's a kind of perfection.

195

Khardung La, so high

Give yourself a fantastic high-mountain adventure in Leh by cycling the Khardung La road north—15 miles (24 km) of asphalt followed by 9 miles (15 km) of trail—taking you ever higher, from 11,500 feet (3,500 m) to 17,500 feet (5,359 m). The summit sign contradicts the GPS measurement, claiming a maximum altitude of 18,380 feet (5,602 m) and the title of "Highest Motorable Pass," but never mind! Simply show your friends a picture of yourself smiling in front of the sign and don't tell them that you were really 880 feet (243 m) lower.

FROM MANALI TO LEH
An extraordinary and demanding high-altitude trek in the north of India

- Manali, **6,726 feet** (2,050 m) > Rohtang La, **13,051 feet** (3,978 m)
- Rohtang La > Koksar, **10,300 feet** (3,140 m)
- Koksar > Keylong, **10,100 feet** (3,080 m)
- Keylong > Bara-lacha La, **16,043 feet** (4,890 m)
- Bara-lacha La > Lachulung La, **16,598 feet** (5,059 m)
- Lachulung La > Taglang La, **17,480 feet** (5,328 m)
- Taglang La > Leh, **11,500 feet** (3,500 m)

Duration
15 days

Distance
300 miles
(480 km)

Difficulty
extreme

Gear
mountain bike

Take the (very) high road *Ladakh, India*

Ladakh—it's the ultimate voyage to the meeting point of three great nations mired in ongoing territorial disputes. For the moment, India retains a fragile authority over Jammu and Kashmir at the expense of China and Pakistan, but Islamabad and Tibet are not so far away. Here, in the disputed far north of India, there lies a magical land for cyclists, one of the most demanding there is: Ladakh. The atmosphere is Tibetan—joyful and colorful—and the horizon is Himalayan. The road that traverses it for 300 miles (480 km) from Manali to Leh, via the monasteries of the valley of the Indus, is considered to be one of the highest in the world. You'll climb and climb. Slowly. And for a long time. Once you get over the Rohtang La Pass, you won't descend below 9,840 feet (3,000 m). Vegetation is only a memory. The key is to acclimatize. Compared to the Galibier and Tourmalet Passes in France, Bara-lacha La, Lachulung La, and Taglang La—all of them at or above 16,000 feet (5,000 m)—are quite something! The road is perfect in some places, atrocious in others. You sleep in tents. The only living things are Bactrian camels, shepherds, and daring truckers dicing with the edge of the precipice. But what a fabulous spectacle!

The Israel National Bike Trail

Jordan's neighbor, Israel, has recently developed a passion for cycling. A national bike trail has been an ongoing project since 2010; it will eventually run all the way from Mount Hermon in the north, bordering Syria, to Eilat in the far south, a distance of over 620 miles (1,000 km)—most of them over rocky trails and paths, requiring the use of mountain bikes. The infrastructure and signage already in place between Eilat and Timna Park are exemplary. Once completed, the trail will make for a fantastic trek, passing through Jerusalem and Tel Aviv.

PETRA HIDES ITS WONDERS

.8 mile
(1.2 km)
length of the Siq,
the narrow gorge
that leads to the
heart of the city

5%
of the city has been
excavated

4,000
tombs still buried,
according to a Japanese
study

20,000
estimated inhabitants
at the height of the
Nabataean kingdom

Magic of the Pink City *Amman to Petra, Jordan*

Jordan is an extraordinary and magical destination. It is quite cyclable, being relatively flat and in the region of 3,200 feet (1,000 m) in altitude. You might be surprised by the chilliness of the air, particularly at night. Petra—one of the most amazing sites on the planet—is a must. If you have ten days, you can travel from the capital, Amman, in the north, all the way south to Aqaba, on the shore of the Red Sea, and back again. Three hundred and seventy miles

(600 km) and two preconditions: check the security situation (it's an unstable region) and book accommodations. There are hotels dotted along the route, although you might also opt for a Bedouin camp for starry nights in Wadi Rum. From Amman and its hills covered with olive trees, you head due south on the King's Highway. Pass the shores of the Dead Sea before reaching Petra, which was hewn from the rock by the Nabataeans 27 centuries ago and is

remarkable not only for its marvels but also for the water conduit system conceived by its founders. You'll never tire of exploring the Pink City, but the astonishing desert landscapes of Wadi Rum, less than 60 miles (100 km) farther south, will beckon you. That's fine. You'll stop at Petra again on the way back.

As extreme as it gets

According to Red Bull, "this mammoth journey across Russia makes the Tour de France look like a walk in the park." The sponsors of the Trans-Siberian Extreme ultra-stage bicycle race are clearly proud of their baby. The race runs from Moscow to Vladivostok and lasts 24 days. The longest of the four stages is 870 miles (1,400 km). The shortest is 250 miles (400 km). There were ten starters in 2015 and 2016. Not all of them finished.

ALL ABOARD THE TRANS-SIBERIAN FOR AN EXTRAORDINARY TRIP

5,958
miles
(9,588 km)
between Moscow
and Vladivostok

7
time zones
crossed between Moscow
and Vladivostok

6
days to reach
Vladivostok from Moscow,
assuming you don't alight

3
extensions to the east
from Lake Baikal: Trans-Manchurian,
Trans-Mongolian, Baikal-Amur

$985
average price
of tickets from Moscow to
Irkutsk and Novosibirsk to
Moscow

Along the Trans-Siberian

Irkutsk to Novosibirsk, Russia

In the languages of Central Asia, from Turkish to Mongol, *cossack* means "free man," someone with no attachments. For centuries, this was the destiny of the soldiers of the steppes. You will need such a state of mind to participate in the crazy bicycle trek from Irkutsk to Novosibirsk: 1,240 miles (2,000 km) straight through Siberia, along the Trans-Siberian. June is the best time to visit, after the snow has melted. Prepare yourself for mosquitoes, a potential visit

by a bear to your bivouac in the icy night, and the permanent danger posed by car and truck drivers on "their" R255 highway. So why visit Siberia, with its straight roads and endless taiga, and the simple meals and quick showers in the basic accommodation that you'll find around Kansk or Krasnoyarsk? It's the charm of Irkutsk, our starting point, close to the extraordinarily clear Lake Baikal; it's the 2,000 feet (600 m) bridge across the Angara River, and the beauty

of the Yenisei River farther on; it's the view of the Altai Mountains, before Novosibirsk; it's the memory of the Cossacks and all those who have suffered in Siberia; it's the original shape of the Novosibirsk train station—it looks like an old locomotive; and it's those unforgettable moments before and after, aboard the Trans-Siberian Express, with your bike safely stowed.

East Timor, a destination to watch

Located 620 miles (1,000 km) east of Bali and north of the Australian coast, Timor is the easternmost island of the main Lesser Sunda Islands. East Timor, half of the territory, has been independent since 2002. This young country will no doubt be a beautiful cycling destination in the near future. The coast is as attractive as that of Bali, the mountains are sumptuous (Tatamailu peaks at 9,797 feet/2,963 m), the road network is decent, and the dry season is very long. Promising.

DESCEND FROM THE MOUNTAIN?
To explore the Ubud region, try a descent of Mount Batur by mountain bike: several companies offer an almost effortless guided tour, from the volcano's summit to the lake of the same name.

2h
distance of the
volcano from Ubud

1
day out for 3h
of mountain biking
(on average)

5,633 feet
(1,777 m)
altitude of Mount Batur

$60
average price
per person

Hidden face *Bali, Indonesia*

Magnificent views, the imposing silhouettes of volcanoes, luxuriant vegetation, welcoming villages, centuries-old temples, terraced rice paddies: this less familiar Bali is neither that of the white sandy beaches of the south coast, nor that of the famous dive spots of the north coast. It's to be discovered by bike, an iconoclastic solution that allows you to take a different approach to exploring the most touristy of the Indonesian islands. An ideal starting point is Gilimanuk on the western tip opposite Java, where West Bali National Park reveals its aquatic treasures. Ride along the jagged, rocky north coast to Lovina Beach, then veer into the interior, toward lakes and mountains. The silhouette of Buyan-Bratan volcano will appear. The lakes of the same names are infinitely beautiful. Farther east, toward Kintamani, lies Batur, another volcano. Here, the road begins to climb. The first of the ancestral temples are within reach, followed by the terraced rice paddies of Tegalalang. Time for a break in Ubud, a surprising city that's a center of contemporary art and yoga—with a sacred monkey forest! The whole journey is 155 miles (250 km) long and can be broken down into four to eight days of riding, fueled by the fresh coconut milk you can buy at the roadside. Your Bali memories will be unlike anyone else's.

The finest of Iran

Journey beyond Anatolia, and you reach Iran—the experience of a lifetime. Forget Teheran; it's too crowded. Start from Isfahan, the former capital of Persia, jewel of that empire, then continue to Yazd, one of the oldest cities in the world, and then Shiraz, a center of art and culture. Next, visit Pasargadae and Persepolis, the ruins of forgotten civilizations. Devote two weeks to these 500 miles (800 km) at 4,900 feet (1,500 m). They are extraordinary.

FROM THE BLACK SEA TO MOUNT ARARAT

- Trabzon, then E 70 > Iyidere
- Iyidere > Ikizdere
- Ikizdere > Sivrikaya
- Sivrikaya > Pazaryolu
- Pazaryolu > Erzurum

- Erzurum, then E 80 > Pasinler
- Pasinler > Horasan
- Horasan > Ağri
- Ağri > Doğubayazit (turn around and return to Erzurum)

Duration
12 to 15 days

Distance
530 miles
(850 km)

Difficulty
medium to
difficult

Gear
mountain bike, to head
off-road now and then

Adventure in Anatolia *Trabzon to the Iranian border, Turkey*

Turkey is twice the size of Germany, so you're spoiled for choices when it comes to picking a cycling destination. How about Eastern Anatolia, far from Ankara, İzmir, Istanbul, and the fertile banks of the Euphrates? It's a tough road to ride, however—one for the experienced cyclist—even if the imams offer tea along the way. Start in Trabzon, on the shores of the Black Sea, following the coast that's already the mountainside. The road is pretty busy, but there's a verge on which you can cycle. Turn off toward İkizdere on a road that's at 2,600 feet (800 m) and where there are ski resorts, just to get an idea of the climate. You'll see the Pontic Mountains appear between pine trees and waterfalls. Erzurum, which has one of the largest universities in Turkey with more than 40,000 students, lies at 6,200 feet (1,900 m); it's the gateway to the east, a land of ancient citadels and sparse steppes. As you proceed, you'll see fewer and fewer trucks, and fewer and fewer

mountain sheep. The grandiose vision of the snow-covered peak of Mount Ararat at 16,854 feet (5,137 m) monopolizes the view to your left. It's a dry, austere region, but there's no question of giving up and failing to reach Doğubayazit and the Ishak Pasha Palace, with its combined Ottoman, Persian, and Armenian architectural styles. Iran is there, 530 miles (850 km) from Trabzon, 12 or 15 days behind you. Return to Erzurum, but with a tailwind from Armenia.

Four miles, nine wineries!

When New Zealanders play rugby, they often teach their opponents a thing or two. The same goes for post match celebrations. The Marlborough vineyards at the end of the Molesworth Road can be toured by way of a Golden Mile bike ride (nearer to four miles, in fact) between the villages of Rapaura and Renwick. There are nine stops, each providing an opportunity to sample wines made from sauvignon and pinot noir. If you make it to at least five wineries in one day, you're a Golden Mile Champion, and you win a prize. Cheers!

FIVE DAYS CYCLING IN NEW ZEALAND
Two options: relaxing (Christchurch to Seddon) or challenging
(Christchurch to Lake Tekapo)

Christchurch

 o--- NORTHWARD ---·--- WESTWARD ---o

Duration
5 days

Difficulty
medium

See
Hanmer Springs
thermal pools
Marlborough vineyards

Distance
205 miles
(330 km)

Distance
155 miles
(250 km)

Difficulty
higher

Duration
5 days

See
Panoramic views over
the Southern Alps
The wild nature of the
Mackenzie District

Sedan | Lake Tekapo

Fascinating South Island *Molesworth, New Zealand*

In the land of the All Blacks, a "station" is a large livestock farm, comparable to an American ranch. Molesworth Station covers 695 square miles (1,800 km²) and supports the country's biggest herd of cattle. Much of the meat is exported to Britain, which has a taste for antipodean beef and lamb. Molesworth, which lies 2,500 miles (4,000 km) from Antarctica and is situated on and around a hilly area blasted by winds from the South Pacific, is also a great place to explore the north of the South Island. The roads snaking between pastures, lakes, and little valleys often offer panoramic views. The light is powerful, the air pure, and the temperatures pleasant. Molesworth Road is a classic, running from Christchurch to Seddon past the famous Marlborough vineyards. The people here are friendly and relaxed. As a cycling town, Christchurch is also the starting point for a trek west, with Mount Cook—New Zealand's highest peak, at 12,218 feet (3,724 m)—in your sights. This idyllic route, lined with oak and plane trees, takes in the Rakaia River and the magnificent Burkes Pass, the gateway to the Southern Alps, before arriving at Lake Tekapo, amid herds of sheep. Two experiences and two sublime approaches to a marvelous country.

Credits

Author's acknowledgements

To Sandrine Salin-Ghilliani, the first close reader, and so much more.

To Jean-Pierre Demenois, Pierre Gouyou Beauchamps, Claude Marthaler,

and all the pedaling globetrotters who inspire us so much.

To Alain Rumpf, François Paoletti, the founders of *200* magazine, Stéphane Hauvette

(who imported the first mountain bike to France), and all those who endlessly reinvent the bicycle.

To Bénédicte, Michelle, and all those who love to explore, meet others, and share, whether on a bike or not.

To Singletrak, Strava, Bicyclette-verte, Mapmyride, and other digital resources that immortalize our rides.

To Singletrack Jamaica for their kind participation.

To Lila, Antonin, Titouan, and Milo, who will continue the journey.